W9-AMT-449

"With much grace, humility, and presence, *Stuck Together* challenges the local church to engage the contentious issues of our time. Using careful scholarship and drawing from deep experience, J. Nelson Kraybill leads us to consider the demands of our life together in Christ for the world. A fresh, timely, wonderfully rich book for those seeking to be Christ's justice amid a broken, violent world."

DAVID FITCH, B. R. Lindner Chair of Evangelical Theology at Northern Seminary and author of *The Church of Us vs. Them: Freedom from a Faith That Feeds on Making Enemies*

"We may be stuck together as families, as churches, as human beings sharing the same world, but can we get unstuck from our polarizing attitudes and behaviors? I'm encouraged to do just that by J. Nelson Kraybill's *Stuck Together*. It's filled with real-life stories of what's gone wrong and how we might move forward in healthier ways, grounded in the example of Jesus and the early church as they, too, faced polarization in their world. There's no quick fix for the deep divide of polarization, but this book points to a better way and offers some practical steps to get there through learning respect for others, listening well, loving our neighbor, and leaning on God."

APRIL YAMASAKI, pastor, editor, and author of *Sacred Pauses: Spiritual Practices for Personal Renewal*

"Polarization, conflict, and violence have become the norm in today's world. But fortunately, some peacemakers offer another path that brings meaning, transformation, and hope to an exhausted globe. In this hopeful and helpful book, J. Nelson Kraybill presents the true stories of peacemakers and the call to remember that we are all in this together. This book is an invaluable resource for the church, with relevant insights and solid religious underpinnings infused with the author's personal experiences—a tool that peacemakers can use to bridge the polarized world."

DR. SAMUEL KEFAS SARPIYA, executive director of the Center for Nonviolence and Conflict Transformation

"Any Christian seeking to hold tension faithfully in these polarized times should read this book. Wise, grace-filled, realistic, and yet deeply hopeful, J. Nelson Kraybill identifies tensions at the core of what it means to be human, tensions that permeate the very text of Scripture itself. Yet these costly tensions can be made beautiful in small ways by our participation in Christ's victory, in resurrection life, and through the outpouring of God's Holy Spirit of self-giving love."

MICHAEL GULKER, president and cofounder of The Colossian Forum

"*Stuck Together* is peppered with insights, anecdotes, and biblical reflections, inviting patience, curiosity, and grace from those on all sides of polarized conversations to regard one another as partners in dialogue rather than as opponents in arms. This book will be a welcome conversation starter for church groups wrestling with what it means to be in communion with those with whom one disagrees."

BETTY PRIES, cofounder and CEO of Credence and author of *The Space Between Us: Conversations about Transforming Conflict*

"In *Stuck Together*, J. Nelson Kraybill embraces a paradox at the heart of the Christian faith. 'The Spirit of God inspired diversity,' he writes, yet 'diversity alone is not an adequate identity for the church.' Thus, the challenge for followers of Jesus is not to agree on everything, but rather to learn how to disagree 'with gentleness and reverence' (1 Peter 3:16). Yet Kraybill does not flinch from naming profound evils, such as genocide against Native Americans and systemic racism, where 'agreeing to disagree' is not an option."

DAVID BRUBAKER, dean of the School of Social Sciences and Professions and professor of organizational studies at Eastern Mennonite University and author of *When the Center Does Not Hold: Leading in an Age of Polarization*

STUCK TOGETHER

STUCK TOGETHER

the HOPE of CHRISTIAN WITNESS
in a POLARIZED WORLD

J. Nelson Kraybill

HERALD
P R E S S

Harrisonburg, Virginia

Herald Press
PO Box 866, Harrisonburg, Virginia 22803
www.HeraldPress.com

Library of Congress Cataloging-in-Publication Data
Names: Kraybill, J. Nelson, author.
Title: Stuck together : the hope of Christian witness in a polarized world
    / J. Nelson Kraybill.
Description: Harrisonburg, Virginia : Herald Press, [2023] | Includes
    bibliographical references and indexes.
Identifiers: LCCN 2022052729 (print) | LCCN 2022052730 (ebook) | ISBN
    9781513810652 (hardcover) | ISBN 9781513810645 (paperback) | ISBN
    9781513810669 (ebook)
Subjects: LCSH: Christian ethics. | Cultural relations--Biblical teaching.
    | Polarization (Social sciences)--Religious aspects--Christianity. |
    Values--Religious aspects--Christianity. | Church and social problems. |
    Witness bearing (Christianity) | Jesus Christ--Example. | BISAC:
    RELIGION / Christian Living / Social Issues | RELIGION / Christian
    Ministry / Discipleship
Classification: LCC BJ1278.A3 K73 2023 (print) | LCC BJ1278.A3 (ebook) |
    DDC 170/.44--dc23/eng/20230105
LC record available at https://lccn.loc.gov/2022052729
LC ebook record available at https://lccn.loc.gov/2022052730

Study guides are available for many Herald Press titles at www.HeraldPress.com.

STUCK TOGETHER
© 2023 by J. Nelson Kraybill
Released by Herald Press, Harrisonburg, Virginia 22803. 800-245-7894.
    All rights reserved.
Library of Congress Control Number: 2022052729
International Standard Book Number: 978-1-5138-1064-5 (paperback);
    978-1-5138-1065-2 (hardcover); 978-1-5138-1066-9 (ebook)
Printed in United States of America

Unless otherwise indicated, scripture quotations are taken from the *New Revised Standard Version*. Copyright © 1989, 1995 National Council of the Churches of Christ in the United States of America. Used by permission. All rights reserved worldwide.

Scripture quotations marked (ESV) are from the *ESV® Bible* (*The Holy Bible, English Standard Version*®), copyright © 2001 by Crossway, a publishing ministry of Good News Publishers. Used by permission. All rights reserved. Scripture quotations marked (KJV) are taken from the *King James Version*. Scripture quotations marked (NIV) are taken from the *Holy Bible, New International Version*®, NIV®. Copyright © 1973, 1978, 1984, 2011 by Biblica, Inc.® Used by permission of Zondervan. All rights reserved worldwide. www.Zondervan.com The "NIV" and "New International Version" are trademarks registered in the United States Patent and Trademark Office by Biblica, Inc.® Scripture marked (NKJV) taken from the *New King James Version*®. Copyright © 1982 by Thomas Nelson, Inc. Used by permission. All rights reserved.

27 26 25 24 23   10 9 8 7 6 5 4 3 2 1

In gratitude for my parents,
Simon Kraybill and Mary Jean Kraybill,
who taught me to follow Jesus
and treat people who differ from me
with respect

CONTENTS

Acknowledgments 11

Foreword 13

Introduction: Today I Fired My Dentist 17

1 Small Actions Can Have Big Consequences 27

2 Boundaries Are Necessary but Can Polarize.......... 39

3 Jesus Also Lived in a Polarized Society 55

4 We Are Lepers in a World That Needs Healing 73

5 Why Jesus and Nicodemus Talked in the Dark........ 87

6 The Big Challenge Is to Listen Well................ 103

7 Our Stories Change How We Read the Bible 119

8 Paul Boldly Bridged the Jew-Gentile Polarity 135

9 Right Remembering Fosters Healing............... 149

10 Systemic Racism Shaped My Neighborhood 165

11 What Draws the Global Church Together?.......... 179

12 Deep Spiritual Wells Can Replenish Hope 195

Conclusion 209

Appendix A: Options for Action.................. 215

*Appendix B: It Matters Where We Get Our News
    and Commentary* 219

Appendix C: Possibilities for Further Reading 221

Index... 223

Notes 227

The Author.................................... 239

ACKNOWLEDGMENTS

A cloud of witnesses gave support and counsel as this book came together. Tim Pebbles spent hours critiquing early concepts, and suggested resources. People who read and responded to all or part of the book as it neared completion include Eleanor Kreider, Mike Yoder, Henk Stenvers, John Hershberger, Frances Ringenberg, Loren Johns, Angela Tanner, John Kampen, Quinn Brenneke, Ben Ollenburger, Shana Peachey Boshart, John Roth, Richard Kauffman, Cyneatha Millsaps, Jesse Carter, César García, Ron Byler, and Tom Yoder Neufeld.

Ellen Graber Kraybill, love of my life, critiqued chapters as they emerged and constantly encouraged. Our daughter Laura Graber Kraybill was a supportive critic and conversation partner throughout. Laura Leonard of Herald Press urged me to submit the proposal for this book, and editor Sherah-Leigh Gerber helped guide my flights of theological reflection to a landing. The entire Herald Press team did much to make this project possible. In addition to Laura and Sherah-Leigh, these include Amy Gingerich, Elisabeth Ivey, Sara Versluis, Reuben Graham, Ardell Stauffer, Eden Fisher, Joe Questel, LeAnn Hamby, and Alyssa Bennett Smith.

While no one named above bears responsibility for short-comings of this book, all helped make it stronger. I am grateful.

—J. Nelson Kraybill
Bethlehem, Palestine
First Week of Advent 2022

FOREWORD

I am honored to write this foreword to this book by my friend J. Nelson Kraybill, with whom I worked closely when he was director of the London Mennonite Centre. I confess that I was not initially inspired by the title, *Stuck Together*. Confronted by destructive and exacerbating polarization in church and society, is this the extent of the hope of Christian witness the subtitle offers? But the more I read, the more apt the title appeared.

Drawing on his insights as a biblical scholar, his experiences as a local pastor, and the global perspectives gained from his role with Mennonite World Conference, Kraybill refuses to make unrealistic claims for what Christian witness can achieve, insisting that salvation is from God. The biblical account of the early church, the history of the Anabaptist-Mennonite tradition, and the struggles of contemporary denominations all testify that polarization, division, and conflict are as problematic within the Christian community as beyond it. If we are to witness with integrity to God's reconciling love and model peaceful practices, we must do so with modesty and humility. Maybe simply sticking together and courageously resisting pressures that threaten to tear us apart is the foundation.

Although he briefly discusses other issues, Kraybill focuses on three topics of particular concern in his North American context: Indigenous rights, racism, and LGBTQ inclusion. But the principles and practices he advocates are applicable to contentious issues in other contexts. When we encounter those whose views are different from ours—views that are maybe even deeply disturbing or offensive to us—we can listen patiently, convey respect, ensure others know we have understood their position, seek to discern their moral foundations, and be slow to condemn. We can seek to avoid labeling, dismissive comments, rancor, and separation. Instead, we can explore gently where we agree and differ, build trust, and choose to remain "stuck together."

None of this means reluctance to name and oppose evil ideologies or systems, nor does it mean eschewing strong convictions. But sticking together means refusing to demonize or anathematize persons. Kraybill notes that the New Jerusalem has walls, but its gates are never closed. Communities need boundaries. For the Christian community, the nonnegotiable foundation is Jesus Christ, but we can remain open to new insights and the hope of reconciled relationships.

Kraybill investigates how the Jewish tradition, in and beyond the Old Testament, handled polarization. He examines the Gospels for examples of how Jesus engaged with polarities in his context. And he illustrates from the book of Acts strategies that enabled the early Christians to remain "stuck together." Although his conclusions may disturb some readers, he argues that disagreement and diversity are normal and can be received as God's gifts to us as stewards and co-creators, inviting us to choose options. Within the Bible there are divergent voices and different approaches on a range of issues. This should not trouble us but rather should encourage us to join the conversation, draw on the riches of past generations, and listen humbly and expectantly to others as we seek to discern the Spirit's leading in our contexts. Reconciliation, not homogenization, is the goal. And the vulnerability and loving bridge-building of Jesus is our model.

"Stuck together" is our identity, a reality to be maintained rather than achieved. The mosaic cross image reminds us of the foundation and cost of this. This book offers us practical wisdom, honesty about mistakes, inspiring examples, biblical resources, spiritual disciplines, and an invitation to "do something" in the hope that small steps can make a real difference in church and society.

—Stuart Murray
Director of the Centre for
Anabaptist Studies and author
of *The Naked Anabaptist*

INTRODUCTION

Today I Fired My Dentist

Just as COVID-19 infections peaked in the United States and tens of thousands were dying, I went to the dentist for a routine checkup. Hygienist Sue, who had cleaned my teeth for years, welcomed me to the dental chair. After brief banter about family and faith (she attends a conservative megachurch), I asked whether she was vaccinated. She blanched and said softly, "No, I am not."

I felt a rush of fear and righteous anger. "I'm sorry, but I cannot be your patient," I said, and rose from the chair. "I want to leave this office as quickly as possible." Sue explained that her family doctor had assured her she did not need a vaccination. "Then you have a quack doctor," I shot back. Sue's next-door neighbor ("a cardiologist!") did not get vaccinated, plus she knew a man who was vaccinated and still ended up in the hospital.

"That's not science," I protested, loudly enough to bring another hygienist to the door. "That's anecdotal evidence, not the way scientists decide anything. That's how wacko commentators on cable news mislead the public: they tell some anecdote, then use that to promote their ideology."

"I totally respect your opinion and your right to choose about vaccinations," Sue responded patiently. "Thank you," I said, "but I do not respect your decision to endanger me and other patients who are unmasked just inches from your face. You could be spreading COVID, and that's irresponsible. What kind of Christian witness is that? You're a good hygienist, but when it came to the great moral test of your career, you decided to go with anecdotal advice and some notion of individual freedom. I will look for a dental practice where they believe in modern science."

On my way out of the office, the receptionist, unmasked and looking grave, offered to send my records to the next dentist. I thanked her and left the office feeling unsettled. Until asked, the hygienist had withheld information that compromised my safety. The situation had blindsided me. I lost my cool.

"When we are surprised, we are most likely to regress," a counselor friend told me later. I had regressed, falling back to a confrontational way of interacting that is not productive. I accused. I implied that the hygienist was stupid for accessing sources of information I consider dubious. I denigrated her Christian faith. "The question for you in that departure from the dental practice," said the counselor, "is, What kind of impression *of you* do you leave with that office?" Oops.

TRIBALISM MAKES POLARITIES UNHEALTHY

Even the jeans we wear have become politicized. Liberals from urban areas typically buy Levi's, allegedly because of that company's progressive stance on gun control and immigration. Conservatives, more likely to be rural, prefer the independent cowboy mystique of Wrangler.[1] Check your wardrobe: Which brand do you wear?

Sociologists say that today there are whole constellations of political, social, and theological positions on both the right and the left of American society.[2] These are clusters of similar ideas and responses that create what in effect are tribal groups. Our tribal affiliation means we are likely to embrace most or all positions of a particular constellation. With other members of our tribe, we tend to share similar convictions regarding vaccine mandates, immigration, government assistance, racial justice, guns, climate change, women's rights, abortion, the integrity of elections, and more. Do you know which is your tribe?

Like most people, my antennae quickly pick up identity cues from others. I reflexively think, "This person is (or is not) from my tribe." Fueling my response to the hygienist was my intuition that she belongs to a tribe whose values I do not share. I still think I made the right decision to change dentists. But I realized later that my abrupt response at least in part grew out of frustration with a whole range of political and theological positions that I assumed the hygienist held. Pigeonholing another person like that was not helpful, and made it less likely that we would learn from each other.

POLARITIES PERCOLATE IN FAMILY, CHURCH, AND COMMUNITY

I held my breath at a weekly family Zoom call when one of my six siblings announced, "Last weekend my spouse and I went with a busload of folks to attend a March for Life at the Pennsylvania state capital." Launching like that into the topic of abortion was either brave or foolhardy. Abortion, just one of a series of contested issues dividing church and society, was daily in the news. The US Supreme Court was about to reverse its 1973 decision allowing abortion, and emotions ran high. Protesters and counterprotesters were facing off in the streets. Bishops were refusing communion to politicians who stepped out of line.

My sibling reported that one speaker at the Pennsylvania March for Life rejoiced that his unwed mother had put him up for adoption instead of getting an abortion. "As a nurse," said my relative, "I concur with biologists who say that life begins at fertilization, and concur with the Bible that says, 'Thou shalt not kill.'" For this sibling, who supports a local pregnancy center, it was an expression of Christian faithfulness to go to the state capitol to advocate for unborn children.

Another sibling spoke up. "This weekend my spouse and I are attending the Women's March for Reproductive Rights in Washington, DC." I tightened my seatbelt and prepared for turbulence. "We also are pro-life," this family member said, with a hint of frustration. "If people who oppose reproductive choice really were pro-life, they would support paid family leave and universal healthcare. They would oppose war and capital punishment. Being created in the image of God means women have the responsibility and right to make decisions about their own bodies. Our bodies are temples for the in-dwelling of God, and decisions about their use should not be made by the state." For this sibling, making those concerns a priority is an expression of Christian faithfulness.

No stormy exchanges followed these remarks, and discussion moved to other topics. We had taken the topic as far as the family could productively go in that setting. Family love prevailed, which is fortunate because we are "stuck together" by DNA and by long shared experience.

You likely have your own polarization stories from family, church, or community. These exchanges do not always end well. Living with love in a fractious world has become a daily challenge for Christians and all members of society. We all find ourselves "stuck together" at work or at school or in the neighborhood with persons we may not like. Even if we avoid the mudslinging of social media and cable news, we feel tension in the air just by attending school board meetings or following current events.

"We are in the grip of a more than fifty year escalating trend of political, cultural, and geographical polarization," says Peter Coleman of Columbia University, "and it is damaging our families, friendships, neighborhoods, workplaces, and communities to a degree not previously seen in our lifetime."[3]

A VISION OF HEALING INSPIRES FOLLOWERS OF JESUS

Our divided world needs more than conflict mediation techniques. Humanity needs Christians—millions of us—to live into God's promise to heal and restore what is broken. I need hope when I let myself get sucked into the maelstrom of polarization in church and society. The apostle Paul speaks of this hope as the "mystery" of God's will, a "plan for the fullness of time, to gather up all things" in Christ, "things in heaven and things on earth" (Ephesians 1:9–10).

The apostle wrestled with painful polarities, especially in relations between Jew and Gentile in the church. When addressing these tensions in his letter to the Ephesians, Paul uses language of far/near, strangers/family, exiles/citizens, and we/you.[4] These terms refer to stresses within the early Christian church but have parallels in church and society today.

Healing such alienation sounds attractive, but at what cost! The divine plan is to "reconcile both groups to God in one body *through the cross*, thus putting to death that hostility through it" (Ephesians 2:16, my emphasis). The apostle does not say exactly how Jesus' suffering and death on the cross bring about reconciliation. But gospel stories show that Christ confronted polarizing powers of greed, hatred, selfishness, and sin with suffering love. He calls his followers to do the same.

When demonic forces answered Jesus' witness with a death sentence, God raised him from the dead, showing that divine love prevails. Jesus' resurrection changed the moral trajectory of history, and all who confess Christ as Lord participate in that great reversal from death to life. If the Spirit that raised Jesus lives in us, Paul declared, it will bring life to our mortal bodies (Romans 8:11). We live as transformed individuals, reconciled to God and participating in God's plan for cosmic reconciliation. We become ambassadors of hope in a polarization-weary world.

JESUS IS OUR MODEL FOR SUSTAINING RELATIONSHIPS
The theology I've described is pretty abstract, which is why the incarnation matters for how we deal with polarization. Theology became tangible when God in Christ showed what it means to be fully human in the divine image. Jesus made himself vulnerable, loving the unlovely and forgiving even those who tried to destroy him. His bridge-building is a model for how we engage polarities today. We follow Jesus because we know wholeness is possible. Divine love and forgiveness restored our relationship with God, and now we extend that grace to the world around us. We live with a global vision of shalom (harmony, wholeness) even if that hope does not come to full fruition in our lifetime.

Followers of Jesus work for reconciliation, not homogenization, in church and society. As we will see, there are unresolved polarities within the Bible itself. These suggest that diversity and disagreement are normal and perhaps necessary for God's people. We can relax a bit and not try to blend all polarities into one stream of conviction. Polarities can productively enliven families and faith communities, and it is possible that people on multiple sides of a given disagreement are living faithfully. They are doing justice, loving mercy, and walking humbly with God (Micah 6:8).

Finding wholeness in a fractured world means we can hold convictions deeply, but humbly. We are fallible creatures who "know only in part," who see only as "in a mirror, dimly." That description of our limited spiritual vision comes from 1 Corinthians 13, the love chapter.

Love is "patient and kind," scripture says (1 Corinthians 13:4), so we take time to respect and hear one another. Not being "arrogant or rude" (13:4–5) means we avoid name-calling and dismissive labeling.

But the apostle Peter assures us that we need not hesitate to share our convictions. "Always be ready to make your defense to anyone who demands from you an accounting for the hope that is in you;" he states, "yet do it with gentleness and reverence" (1 Peter 3:15–16). The world should know Christians by our gracious hope, not by judgmentalism or sarcasm. If Christians do no more than engage those with whom we disagree with gentleness and reverence, it will make a difference in the world.

CURIOSITY AND HOPE INSPIRED THIS BOOK

This is a book on living into a vision of wholeness in a divided world, not a step-by-step handbook on conflict transformation.[5] Reconciling efforts that you and I make will not end all polarization in church or society any more than being a pacifist will end all wars. On a macro level, most of us have little or no control over tensions between nations or between whole sectors of society. But on a micro level, we can some-times effect change. Even when we are in a nation at war or a society with corrosive polarization, Christians can bear testi-mony to "a more excellent way" (1 Corinthians 12:31).

I began writing these chapters with questions in mind, including curiosity about the following:

- *The Bible:* What attitude does the Bible take toward polarities in the Jewish or Christian faith communities? What wholeness did God's people find amid inter-nal conflict?
- *Jesus:* How did Jesus function in polarized Palestine? What were the religious or political options that he faced for dealing with religious or political fragmentation?
- *The early church:* How did visionary Christian leaders of the early centuries work at reconciling polarities within and beyond the church?
- *The church today:* What does it mean to belong to a stressed denomination, and how do we relate to the global Christian church?

The first enduring insight that emerged for me in this study is how contrasting perspectives enrich faith communities when people listen well, communicate in loving ways, and share underlying convictions. The Bible, the ancient Jewish com-munity, and the early church all give examples of such unity in diversity. We should expect and even welcome variation in church and society today so long as we have a hub of shared convictions at the center.

A second enduring insight speaks to the mission of the church: God's plan to unite all things in Christ means we can joyfully dedicate ourselves to building trust and com-munication between polarized groups both in church and in society. Faithful witness allows us to have deep convictions *and* reach beyond comfortable circles of like-minded people to learn from other perspectives, including other world religions and philosophies.

BE GRACIOUS BUT DO NOT REMAIN SILENT

Nothing in this book should diminish the importance of naming and opposing malevolent forces of racism, economic exploitation, and other evils that warp humanity. Christians must not politely acquiesce to environmental degradation, arms proliferation, or sexual abuse to attain "peace." If we do not name and confront disinformation or violation of basic human rights, the prophet Jeremiah's judgment will be upon us: "They have treated the wound of my people carelessly, saying 'Peace, peace,' when there is no peace" (Jeremiah 6:14). Reconciliation does not mean harmony at any cost.

Even Jesus, model of reconciliation, asked, "Do you think that I have come to bring peace to the earth? No, I tell you, but rather division!" The gospel will turn "father against son and son against father, mother against daughter and daughter against mother" (Luke 12:51, 53). Jesus here alludes to a scathing passage in Micah (6:9–7:7) about economic, judicial, and moral rot in Israel. Micah says the "wealthy are full of violence" (6:12) and cheat at business. People "lie in wait for blood" (7:2) and manipulate with bribes. The powerful "dictate what they desire" and "pervert justice" (7:3).

There are times when speaking the truth about such evil explodes relationships, and Good Friday was such a conflagration. Decades earlier, Simeon had told Jesus' mother Mary that her child was "destined for the falling and the rising of many in Israel" (Luke 2:34). Truth-telling for the gospel can unsettle others, but Jesus still often showed respect and love even toward those who would destroy him. Our challenge is to engage polarized situations with the same combination of courage and love.

THE FLOW OF THIS BOOK

In the following chapters, I present no grand scheme of my own to save either church or society from destructive polarization. Salvation belongs to God. But with Bible study, insight from the social sciences, and many stories, this book explores

1. Reasons to take even small steps toward healing relationships (chapter 1)
2. How the Old Testament and Jewish tradition handled polarization (chapter 2)
3. Surprising ways Jesus, Paul, and the early church overcame division (chapters 3–6)
4. Biblical insight on divisions over sexuality, White supremacy, and more (chapters 7–11)
5. Spiritual disciplines that sustain our hope (chapter 12)

At the end of each chapter is a list of questions for reflection and discussion. Appendix A suggests options for action. Appendix B highlights issues Christians might consider in choosing news and opinion sources. Appendix C lists possibilities for further reading. There is also a general index of names and topics.

This book can serve well for individual reflection, sermon preparation, small group discussion, or adult education classes. May ideas presented here inspire your continuing participation in God's holy work of healing our polarized world.

1

SMALL ACTIONS CAN HAVE BIG CONSEQUENCES

Before we jump into the deep end of the polarization pool, let's pause for a story about small actions having big consequences. If we are going to take daily steps toward healing a polarized world, we need hope that God can use even our modest actions to make changes—first in ourselves, then perhaps in others.

One summer night when I was a child, thieves were helping themselves to gasoline from a tank that supplied tractors on the family farm in Pennsylvania where I was raised. Such theft had happened before, but this time Dad was prepared. He had stretched a fishline across the driveway entrance and all the way to my parents' bedroom, where he tied the end to an alarm clock. The alarm sounded around midnight and Dad jumped out of bed. He slipped out of the darkened house and sneaked up on the crime scene.

Sure enough, a young man was pumping fuel while his buddies waited inside their car. Hoping to get a license number, Dad switched on his flashlight and greeted the startled visitors.

The car—its license plate bent double to hide the number—lurched into gear and sped away. Left behind, the chap pumping gas disappeared down half-mile-long rows of tall corn.

Days later, while delivering produce to stores in nearby villages, Dad recognized the offending car parked on a street in Elizabethtown. A crease in the license plate confirmed his suspicions, and he soon found the owners nearby. As was customary for Dad, he made amiable small talk with the lads before getting around to his agenda: Where were you fellows last Friday night?

When the young men said they had never been near the Kraybill farm, Dad offered them a chance to see the place. Could they come immediately? There would be ice cream. Flustered or bemused by the unexpected kindness, the lads had no reason to say no. A car filled with town boys soon followed Dad out to the farm, where Mother set out dessert.

When the ice cream was gone, Dad told the guests that he was quite certain they had stolen gasoline and was concerned about where such conduct would lead them. If they needed gas that badly, they should just ask, and he would fill their tank. (One lad did come back later to take up the offer.) Without admitting wrongdoing, the boys left—and under one plate was a five-dollar bill, enough to buy a tank of gas at 1950s prices.

CAN ICE CREAM RECONCILIATION AFFECT GLOBAL POLARIZATION?

What could that perfect-ending small-town incident have to do with great polarizations in the world today? It's one thing to show a simple act of kindness toward local boys stealing gas because their brains or consciences were not fully developed. It's another to deal with conflicts that splinter churches or lead to war between nations.

I was too young to be aware of the gas theft when it happened, but the story took root in our family's oral tradition and became part of how we seven children viewed the world. My parents didn't make a big deal of it, and I didn't think of it as faith formation. It was just another example of Dad's wit. But later I learned biblical connections:

> If your enemies are hungry, give them bread to eat;
>> and if they are thirsty, give them water to drink;
> for you will heap coals of fire on their heads,
>> and the LORD will reward you. (Proverbs 25:21–22)

Hebrew sages may have borrowed the coals of fire image from an ancient Egyptian ritual of carrying hot coals on the head as a sign of contrition.[1] Regardless of the origin of the metaphor, the apostle Paul cites it as a way to "overcome evil with good" (Romans 12:20–21). Being generous ultimately did not spare Paul from martyrdom at Rome. But ice cream made our gas thieves contrite enough to pay for what they had stolen, and years later one came back and apologized.

WE RESPOND TO POLARIZATION BY "PATIENT FERMENT"

It takes a change of heart and a change of culture to be kind to persecutors and love enemies. How do followers of Jesus learn such countercultural responses? Church historian Alan Kreider writes about the "patient ferment" of early Christians, who quietly taught and lived the way of Jesus in an empire entrenched in idolatry, materialism, and violence.[2] Though few in number, Christians became leaven in society because they developed new habits and new reflexes shaped by the Hebrew Prophets and the teaching of Jesus. Christian faith grew almost imperceptibly in the Roman Empire as networks of love, forgiveness, and hope quietly pervaded the pagan world. Followers of Jesus today will address polarization the same way, usually with small and consistent actions.

Early Christians often cited two Bible passages they had committed to memory: the mountain of the Lord passage (Isaiah 2:2–4) and the Sermon on the Mount (Matthew 5–7). Countercultural phrases abound in these passages. Nations beat swords into plowshares and do not learn war anymore. Merciful people and peacemakers receive blessing, alienated brothers and sisters reconcile. Followers of Jesus turn the other cheek when slapped, love their enemies, and pray for persecutors. They do not store up treasures on earth and do not judge others. Memorization and regular use of these passages shaped early believers and rewired their behavior—something that, more recently, the Amish have also demonstrated.

THE LORD'S PRAYER SHAPES AMISH MORAL REFLEXES

After the massacre of five girls and wounding of five others at a rural Amish schoolhouse in Pennsylvania in 2006, the Amish community received global attention for its quick move to forgive. The killer had died by his own hand, but the Amish community—though reeling from grief—reached out in love to his family. Historian Steven Nolt tells how the Amish explain this counterintuitive response:

> They immediately point to Jesus' parables on forgiveness and especially to the Lord's Prayer, with its key line: Forgive us as we forgive others. This phrase rings loudly in Amish ears because they pray the Lord's Prayer frequently. It's not uncommon in the Lancaster, Pennsylvania, settlement for Amish people to pray the Lord's Prayer eight times a day, and ten times on Sundays.[3]

"Our Father in heaven," Jesus taught his followers to pray, "forgive us our debts, as we also have forgiven our debtors." Nolt says the Amish also quote Jesus' words that immediately follow: "For if . . . you do not forgive others, neither will your Father forgive your trespasses" (Matthew 6:15). Memorized and repeated within a supportive faith community, such teaching builds resilience and shapes reflexes that orient the Amish in daily life.[4]

A Jewish man became Christian and joined the small Anabaptist church to which my family and I belonged in London, England. He once asked with a note of frustration, "Why don't you Christians know the teachings of your rabbi?" Having been raised Jewish, he knew that members of a faith community had to internalize essential teachings of their tradition to maintain vitality. Most Christians profess to value the Sermon on the Mount, but why is the whole of it not on the tip of our tongues?

A LITTLE BOX AT THE DOORWAY HELPS SHAPE MY IDENTITY

Attached to the doorframe at the front entrance to our home is a small rectangular box called a mezuzah, meaning "doorpost" in Hebrew. I bought the mezuzah in Israel, and I touch it when I pass through the doorway. A small scroll inside contains words I repeat, "Hear, O Israel: The LORD is our God, the LORD alone. You shall love the LORD your God with all your heart, and with all your soul, and with all your might" (Deuteronomy 6:4–5).

Observant Jews have mezuzahs on doorways throughout their homes because Deuteronomy 6 says they should bind those words to their hands, fix them to their foreheads, and write them on the doorposts of their houses. Moses probably did not expect God's people to take his instruction so literally, but touching that mezuzah daily affects my spiritual life. Greed, lust, and political polarization tug at my allegiance. I need to be reminded to love the Lord with heart, soul, and might—and to follow Jesus, who added the instruction "Love your neighbor as yourself."

SMALL CHANGES CAN BRING BIG RESULTS

Author James Clear has studied habits for decades, and his Habits Academy has trained thousands of people to quit or establish habits—everything from stopping procrastination to exercising regularly. In his 2018 book *Atomic Habits: Tiny Changes, Remarkable Results*, Clear likens a small change in habits to a small adjustment in the heading of an aircraft:

> Imagine you are flying from Los Angeles to New York City. If a pilot . . . adjusts the heading just 3.5 degrees south, you will land in Washington, D.C., instead of New York. Such a small change is barely noticeable at takeoff—the nose of the airplane moves just a few feet—but when magnified across the entire United States, you end up hundreds of miles apart.[5]

Changing even small habits can make a big difference in the long haul, much like compound interest. However, Clear says, for a change of habit to persist, it often requires us to make a change in our *identity*. When a person who wishes to quit smoking is offered a cigarette, for example, they may have to do more than just say, "No thanks, I'm trying to quit" (a change of behavior). They are more likely to successfully drop the habit if they say, "No, thanks, I'm not a smoker."

That's a change of identity. For Christians in a polarized world who want to be part of God's plan to unite all things in Christ, we might need to say, "I am a follower of Jesus Christ who shows respect and love as he did, even toward people I do not like."

EARLY CHRISTIANS WORSHIPED AND LEARNED IN HOUSEHOLD SETTINGS

Early Christians typically met in private homes, where they gathered weekly to share what Alan Kreider calls the "evening banquet." In that setting, Christians feasted, learned scripture, encouraged each other, and became family—sisters and brothers in Christ. Worship and fellowship happened in these domestic settings, and a variety of persons were present: women, men, children, elderly, enslaved servants, freeborn, rich, poor, Gentiles, and Jews. Social, economic, and political barriers broke down as Christian households hosted a meal.

Spiritual and political implications of the gospel became tangible at these meals in ways that were formative for all participants, including children. Upper-class people who came to the table learned the values of a community that did not seat people by social rank. Whether poor or rich, believers learned to share life and worship with those different from themselves.[6] Such change of behavior was not always easy or complete, since ingrained habits are difficult to change.

BACKGROUND AND LIFE EXPERIENCES SHAPE OUR INTUITIVE RESPONSES

Social psychologist Jonathan Haidt helps explain why ingrained beliefs and behavior resist change, leading to polarization. The title of his book communicates a lot: *The Righteous Mind: Why Good People Are Divided by Politics and Religion.* Multiple studies have convinced Haidt and other researchers that most of us make ethical and moral choices based on convictions which lie so deep within us that we act on them by *intuition*—gut feelings—rather than by conscious decision. "We find ourselves liking or disliking something the instant we notice it," Haidt says, "sometimes before we even know what it is."[7] Factors shaping such deep intuition may include family background, life experiences, education, and even our genes.

Picture an elephant with a human rider guiding the beast. Haidt compares the elephant to the *intuition* we all experience when we make moral choices. The elephant—our gut feeling—has overwhelming strength and usually determines the direction it will go. The rider is our *conscious thinking* when we make moral choices. The rider may try to steer but is weaker than the elephant, which has 90 percent of the power.

As elephant and rider encounter moral choices, the elephant begins to lean one way or the other before the rider even has a chance to respond. Most of the time the rider just goes along. If pressed, the rider likely will offer explanations for decisions *already made* by the elephant of intuition. Once we have made our moral choices, Haidt says, we then are likely to seek out the company of others who share our perspectives. We go to social media sites or to churches that agree with us to reinforce our gut feelings on a range of topics. We become polarized.

Haidt says we do moral decision-making in six categories that he calls moral foundations. Each of these foundations has both positive and negative expression. Using Haidt's titles for the foundations, I summarize them as follows:

- *Care/harm*: concern for the pain of others and responding with compassion
- *Fairness/cheating*: concern for justice, rights, and equity
- *Authority/subversion*: concern for traditions, institutions, and values

- *Loyalty/betrayal*: fidelity to group, institution, or nation
- *Sanctity/degradation*: commitment to what is noble, elevated, or pure
- *Liberty/oppression*: concern for freedom from domination or control

Social scientists using moral foundations theory say that most of us primarily function out of just part of this list. Here are brief examples of how we might apply that insight:

- Many theological and political liberals emphasize concerns of the care/harm and fairness/cheating foundations. These persons are likely to advocate for *care* of the vulnerable (such as minorities or single parents) and *fairness* in structures of society (such as people with higher income paying more taxes, or economically disadvantaged people having adequate legal representation in court).
- Many theological and political conservatives build on the loyalty/betrayal, authority/subversion, and sanctity/degradation foundations. These persons are likely to promote *loyalty* to traditional institutions (such as government, church, family), respect for *authority* (perhaps expressed as "law and order"), and elements of *sanctity* (such as respect for the national flag or for the Ten Commandments).

Exploring Haidt's six moral foundations in detail is beyond the scope of this book. It is useful for our study, however, to keep in mind that humans so habitually operate within our preferred moral categories that it may be difficult to understand or appreciate someone who operates with a set of moral foundations different from our own.

UNDOCUMENTED IMMIGRANTS AND ABORTION
REVEAL OUR MORAL FOUNDATIONS

Consider this example of how moral foundations theory illu-
minates the current polarization over the way American society responds to undocumented immigrants. My wife Ellen and
I belong to a congregation that welcomes immigrants, many
of whom come across the border from Latin America without papers. Ellen and I speak Spanish and find joy in building
friendship with people from different cultures.

Political liberals like us are likely to draw on the *care* moral
foundation to support people from nations enduring violence
and poverty. Out of *fairness* we also might argue that most
North Americans have immigrant ancestors and so should be
sympathetic to newcomers. Political conservatives may also
be caring people, but their concern for legitimate *authority*
would make them less likely to support immigrants who arrive
illegally. A healthy society needs both the liberal impulse to
show compassion and the conservative impulse to maintain
order. North Americans may simply have to live with tension
between *care* for undocumented arrivals and *authority* to
enforce proper legal entry.

Moral foundations theory can also illuminate debates
over abortion. Conservatives appeal to the *sanctity* of
human life even in the womb. Liberals appeal to the need
for people to have *liberty* to make choices about their own
bodies. Many people in debates over abortion, immigration,
and other contested issues base their convictions on valid
moral criteria. Trouble arises when people appeal to different moral foundations and then accuse opponents of racism,
misogyny, selfishness, or some other undesirable trait. We
or others might actually be operating out of such undesirable motives, but we do well to listen carefully for the moral

foundations of persons with whom we disagree before we judge or condemn.]

GENERATIONS RETELL A STORY OF RECONCILIATION

This chapter began by asking how a charming tale about gas thieves in a quiet farming community could be relevant for dealing with great polarizations of the world. It turns out that my father's creative response in that situation made an impact on generations. When Dad died in 2021 at age ninety-nine, my brother Ron said at the funeral,

> The most important narrative of my childhood, aside from the Bible stories that set the foundation for everything, was the story of Daddy and the Gas Thieves. . . I heard this story many times as a child. I don't recall any preaching about it. But I knew that it had everything to do with following Jesus. This was how we were meant to respond to evil in the world; this is how we bear witness to a new way of living.

Ron went on to a lifetime of conflict mediation work around the world, including a stint as a United Nations diplomat. He told the gas thieves story "on every continent." Our niece Sheryl Keller is an elementary school educator. She said, "Each of the fifteen years I was in the classroom, I shared the gas thieves story with my students, and watched their surprise at the unexpected and undeserved grace. Grandpa lived out his faith, treating others as we would like to be treated."

Chapter 1

REFLECT AND DISCUSS

1. Do you have life experience stories (whether positive or negative) from childhood or later that influence how you act in situations of wrongdoing, conflict, or polarization?

2. What moral choices does the elephant (intuition) make for you, and what choices does the rider (your conscious mind) make? What does or should shape your intuition?

3. What Bible verses, prayers, or spiritual resources mold your reflexes for responding to conflict? What influences from the world around you run counter to the way of Jesus?

4. What questions does this chapter raise for you?

BOUNDARIES ARE NECESSARY *but* CAN POLARIZE

Who belongs in my group? What ideas or people does my group accept or endorse? What or whom do we reject? These questions are common in faith communities, and they sometimes intensify polarization in church and society today.

Ecstasy surged through Jewish worshipers in the sixth century BC when they finally returned to Jerusalem after seventy years of exile in Babylon:

> When the LORD restored the fortunes of Zion,
> we were like those who dream.
> Then our mouth was filled with laughter,
> and our tongue with shouts of joy. (Psalm 126:1–2)

God's people were back in the city of David. But along with jubilation came hard questions about boundaries for the restored faith community. Should persons with no Jewish background—specifically, Canaanite wives of Jewish men—be part of the redeemed people? The Hebrew Bible was still in formation, but leaders of the restored Jerusalem looked to these emerging texts for guidance.

Christians today commonly expect scripture to inform our attitudes and practices regarding science, abortion, sexuality, and more. But using scripture to address such matters brings conflicting interpretations and, in some cases, division in the body of Christ. The very Bible to which we go for guidance contains a range of perspectives on many matters of faith and practice.

The sixty-six books of the Bible include contrasting understandings on topics such as the relationship between Jews and Gentiles, the validity of monarchy, and the reason suffering happens. On certain questions, such as participation in war, it's impossible to say, "This is *the* biblical answer." The Spirit of God inspired diversity. There are limits to this diversity, but ours is an expansive God whose people have often embodied a wide range of beliefs and practices.

INTERNAL TENSIONS CAN BENEFIT HEALTHY COMMUNITIES

In vibrant faith communities some internal tension is normal, as happens in the arts. Music often features patterns of repetition that feel predictable until dissonant notes, key changes, or other dynamics interrupt. Changes create tension that moves the music forward toward resolution. The music may return to its starting point or finish at a different place, but without creative disruption the piece would be bland.

Healthy faith communities experience something similar. Tradition establishes comfortable patterns of repetition. Then dissonance (something not in harmony) or syncopation (something not in the same rhythm) creates tension. The unexpected dynamic can feel chaotic but will usually resolve either by returning to the original pattern (tradition) or by landing at a new equilibrium (innovation).

In the church it is natural to wish that the chaotic middle movement of this process would end quickly. But sometimes it takes years or even centuries for God's people to decide a disputed matter. In early centuries of the church, for example, there were conflicting opinions regarding which writings should have the status of scripture.

The church did not decide this matter until the fourth century.[1] There were three hundred years of disagreement and varying practice. The fact that church history and the Bible itself reflect this kind of protracted internal tension should reassure us. Perhaps we, too, can live with substantial differences without expecting whole congregations or denominations to quickly reach unanimity.

EZRA BRINGS TORAH INSTRUCTION AND MAKES PAINFUL CHOICES

Tensions over how to define boundaries of the faith community go back at least to the time of Ezra, who attempted to legislate a kind of ethnic and theological uniformity in Jerusalem. A generation after Babylon destroyed Jerusalem in 586 BC and took many Jews into exile, Babylon itself fell to the Persians, who allowed the exiles to return home. God's people migrated back to Jerusalem in several waves. The first who returned laid foundations for a rebuilt temple (Ezra 3:8–13) and awaited a restored Jewish monarchy. But most returnees apparently knew little about the Torah—the Law of Moses, the first five books of our Old Testament.

Among scholars still in Babylon was a scribe named Ezra, a teacher skilled in the Torah. The "gracious hand of his God was upon him" (Ezra 7:9), and he learned of the need for

Torah instruction in Jerusalem. He had enough clout with the Persians to organize a state-funded mission to take Torah scriptures to his fellow Jews in Jerusalem (7:7–28).

After joining worship at Jerusalem, Ezra heard unsettling reports that men of the Jewish community there had married women who were Canaanite, Hittite, Moabite, Egyptian, or of other foreign extraction. The "holy seed" was being mingled with foreign blood (Ezra 9:1–2). When Nehemiah arrived later from Babylon to rebuild the city walls, he was not subtle in rebuking Jewish men for taking foreign wives. "I contended with them and cursed them and beat some of them and pulled out their hair," he said (Nehemiah 13:25).

There were biblical reasons to reject such marriages. According to Deuteronomy, before Israelites entered Canaan, Moses had said,

> Make no covenant with [the people of Canaan] and show them no mercy. Do not intermarry with them, . . . for that would turn away your children from following me, to serve other gods. . . . No Ammonite or Moabite shall be admitted to the assembly of the LORD. Even to the tenth generation, none of their descendants shall be admitted, . . . because they did not meet you with food and water on your journey out of Egypt, and because they hired against you Balaam . . . to curse you. (Deuteronomy 7:2–4; 23:3–4)

Ezra publicly confessed his people's sin of disobedience and ordered all of Judah to convene in Jerusalem or face property confiscation. On a cold and rainy day, this sorry crowd shivered in an open courtyard in front of the temple (Ezra 10). Ezra told the assembly that they had compounded their sin by marrying Gentile women. The men repented and sent their

Canaanite wives away with their children, an expulsion that feels brutal to modern sensibilities.

LIKE EZRA, THE CHURCH FACES BOUNDARY QUESTIONS TODAY

There may be little parallel in the Western church today for such faith-induced divorce, but it still occurs in some situations of polygamy in sub-Saharan Africa. Some African Independent Churches, seeing how polygamy is taken for granted in the Old Testament, have received members in polygamous unions. For other Christian denominations in Africa, however, the practice raises boundary questions. If a polygamous man becomes a Christian, for example, must he abandon all wives but one and send the rest away?

Western churches have had their own experience with boundary-setting. Not long ago many denominations viewed divorce as a disqualifying moral failure. The church of my childhood disciplined women who cut their hair and anyone who owned a television. In some churches today, those who take the wrong position on abortion, homosexuality, or even political party affiliation face formal or informal exclusion.

In our polarized environment, both liberal and conservative churches can marginalize persons who dissent from community norms. People at both ends of the liberal-conservative spectrum can cite Bible verses and theological rationale for rejecting contrary perspectives. The Bible *should* be a guide for faith and practice, but which passages do we choose, and how do we interpret them?

Ezra presumably relied on teaching from Deuteronomy when he exhorted Jewish men to divorce. But strains of theology within the Hebrew Bible reflect other attitudes toward community boundaries. Two small books, which likely appeared in writing during or shortly after the Babylonian exile, offer perspectives in contrast to Ezra and Nehemiah.

THE BOOK OF JONAH CHALLENGES EXCLUSIVE NATIONALISM

Full of wit and satire, the book of Jonah features a nationalistic Jewish prophet whom God summons to preach to the enemies of Israel. God calls Jonah to go to Nineveh, capital of the Assyrian Empire that had destroyed the northern kingdom of Israel. But instead of going to Nineveh, Jonah boards a ship headed in the opposite direction.

A terrible storm batters the boat, which the crew blames on the moral failure of a yet-to-be identified passenger. Casting lots to locate the culprit, the sailors suspect Jonah. He admits his disobedience to God and suggests that they pitch him overboard to appease heaven. The sailors comply, the seas stop raging, and Jonah becomes lunch for a large fish. In the belly of that fish Jonah prays for three days until the creature spews him onto dry land.

Now at last the reluctant prophet goes to Nineveh. He walks through the wicked city announcing that it is about to be overthrown. Astonishingly, people of Nineveh turn to God and repent with fasting and sackcloth. The king orders even *animals* to wear sackcloth and mandates that his people turn from evil and violence. National conversion happens in a nation that terrorized the ancient world. With Nineveh in full repentance, God decides not to destroy the city after all.

At this point humor turns to sarcasm, and the storyteller describes Jonah complaining because Nineveh had repented. *I told you this would happen,* Jonah groans. *God is so merciful that I just knew this would happen if I preached in Nineveh!*

Jonah had reason to be angry. In obedience to God, he had publicly warned that Nineveh was about to be overthrown. Then God changed plans and saved the city, making Jonah look like a false prophet. In his misery Jonah seeks shelter from a torrid sun, and God provides shade with a bush. Then, as if tweaking the prophet, God "appointed a worm" (Jonah 4:7) to infest the bush and make it wither. The poor man is so distraught that he wishes to die.

Imagine Jewish people who had endured the painful expulsion of family members with Gentile ancestry hearing the story of Jonah. The narrative ends with God reprimanding the prophet:

> You are concerned about the bush, for which you did not labor and which you did not grow; it came into being in a night and perished in a night. And should I not be concerned about Nineveh, that great city, in which there are more than a hundred and twenty thousand persons . . . ? (Jonah 4:10–11)

Regardless of when exactly the book of Jonah appeared, it is in our Bibles along with Ezra and Deuteronomy. If God was ready to save even the people of Nineveh, why would God not want Jewish men to bring Canaanite wives into the faith community at Jerusalem?

THE STORY OF RUTH TRANSCENDS ETHNIC BOUNDARIES

The book of Ruth, which also probably appeared in writing around the time of Ezra and Nehemiah, gives another counterpoint to Deuteronomy's harsh stance on foreign spouses. This author uses romance rather than satire to address boundary issues. The story of Ruth takes place more than five hundred years before Ezra's era and may have been in the oral tradition for centuries. It tells of a Jewish couple named Naomi and Elimelech who lived in Bethlehem when judges ruled the nation. Famine impels them to move to Moab on the far side of the Dead Sea, where they raise two sons. But tragedy strikes when Elimelech dies, followed by the death of both sons, who had grown up to marry Moabite women. This leaves Naomi widowed, an Israelite in a foreign land, with two Moabite daughters-in-law.

Israelites had a list of reasons to despise Moab, starting with belief that the founder of the Moabite nation was the product of incest (Genesis 19:30–37). The king of Moab once hired the seer Balaam to curse Israelites when they were on their way from Egypt to Canaan, and Moabite women allegedly lured Israelite men into adultery (Numbers 25). Moses had declared that no Moabite should enter the assembly of the Lord (Deuteronomy 23:3). Amos, Isaiah, Jeremiah, Ezekiel, and Zephaniah all heap scorn or curses upon Moab. Psalm 108:8–9 portrays God saying, "Judah is my scepter. Moab is my washbasin; on Edom I hurl my shoe."

With such vitriol in Israelite culture, we might expect Naomi's migration from Bethlehem to Moab to be a tale of rejection. Instead, she and her family apparently enjoy a gracious reception. Her sons marry Moabite women, one being Ruth, who eventually moves to Bethlehem when Naomi returns home. Before leaving Moab, Naomi urges Ruth not to accompany her back to Bethlehem. But Ruth responds with tender words, "Do not press me to leave you or to turn back from following you! Where you go, I will go; where you lodge, I will lodge; your people shall be my people, and your God my God" (Ruth 1:16).

Ruth had evidently converted from pagan religion to faith in Yahweh: *Your God will be my God.* The Israelite community at Bethlehem warmly receives Ruth, and an Israelite landowner marries her. From that union comes a son named

Obed, grandfather of King David. The book of Ruth culminates by highlighting King David's Moabite ancestry, suggesting that his Gentile roots are significant to the meaning of the whole story (Ruth 4:13–22). The greatest king of Israel had a Moabite great-grandmother. The early church also celebrated Ruth the outsider by naming her as an ancestor of Jesus (Matthew 1:5).

Imagine the story of Ruth circulating in Jerusalem at the time Ezra and Nehemiah were condemning marriage to Canaanites. "What about the great-grandmother of King David?" someone could ask. "Would we have expelled Ruth?"

The prophet Isaiah would have welcomed Ruth, as we see in his call for inclusion. Moses had sternly prohibited foreigners and eunuchs from participating in the faith community (Deuteronomy 23:1), but Isaiah shows God welcoming them:

> To the eunuchs who keep my sabbaths,
> who choose the things that please me
> and hold fast my covenant,
> I will give . . . an everlasting name
>   that shall not be cut off.

> And the foreigners who join themselves to the LORD,
> to minister to him, . . .
> and to be his servants . . .
> these I will bring to my holy mountain, . . .
> for my house shall be called a house of prayer
> for all peoples. (Isaiah 56:4–7)

DEUTERONOMY GIVES MIXED MESSAGES ON BOUNDARIES

Any Israelite wanting to argue for inclusion of Canaanites could argue that the Torah itself is not of one mind regarding boundaries for foreigners. Deuteronomy celebrates the fact that Yahweh is a God "who executes justice for the orphan and the widow, and who loves the strangers [foreigners], providing them food and clothing." Because of God's gracious character, even Moses declares, "You shall also love the stranger, for you were strangers in the land of Egypt" (Deuteronomy 10:18–19).

Alongside an abundance of such humane teaching, passages in Deuteronomy prescribe merciless treatment of other peoples. "You shall annihilate them—the Hittites and the Amorites, the Canaanites and the Perizzites, the Hivites and the Jebusites . . . so that they may not teach you to do all the abhorrent things that they do for their gods" (Deuteronomy 20:17–18). The rationale for this brutality apparently was to guard Israelites against idolatry. That seems meager justification for genocide, and in fact the Israelites did not always follow the harsh directive.

In ancient Middle Eastern cultures, armies commonly put defeated peoples or cities under the "ban" (*herem*). This meant that victors would sacrifice some of or all their war booty—including prisoners of war—to gods who had granted triumph.[2] We see Israelites (mostly) implementing such a ban in their conquest of Ai (Joshua 7–8). But it is possible that the ban, which underscored that victory belongs to God, had more symbolic than literal meaning. If Israelites during conquest had annihilated all other people groups, their presence in later generations would have been reduced. Perhaps prescribing the ban was a way of saying *Take categorical, even extreme, measures to guard against idolatry.*

Both the exclusive approach of Ezra toward foreigners and the inclusive approach of Ruth and Jonah appear in our Bible. To sustain such diversity, God's people had to have underlying shared convictions that held the community together. The most important shared conviction was monotheism, faith in Yahweh alone as true God.[3]

The specific reason Moses told the Israelites never to marry a Canaanite was because such unions might import pagan religion. But there is no hint that Ruth introduced foreign gods or idolatry into Israel. Ruth converted to Yahwistic faith when she moved to Bethlehem. When a storm threatened to sink Jonah's ship, Jonah told the crew that he was a Yahweh worshiper, and they also believed. Even people of wicked Nineveh ended up turning to God.

CHANGE MAY NEED TO HAPPEN GRADUALLY

Faith communities often accept change only years or decades after the shift begins, and the lag may be a good thing. Devout conservatives at Bethlehem would have had ample reason to express concern about the marriage of Boaz and Ruth. Unless traditionalists upheld biblical teaching in such situations, the faith community could cut loose from confessional moorings.

During the centuries after Ruth married Boaz, considerable evidence emerged that intercultural marriage was either the cause or the effect of disobedience. King Solomon's foreign wives "turned away his heart after other gods" (1 Kings 11:4). When King Ahab married Phoenician princess Jezebel, he "went and served Baal" (16:31). But despite this sorry record, people in Israel who accepted intercultural marriage still could build their case by pointing to Ruth the Moabite in King David's ancestry.

The Hebrew prophets reflect their own polarities of attitude toward foreigners. Isaiah and Micah foresee a time when all nations will stream toward Jerusalem. Foreign peoples will say, "Come, let us go up to the mountain of the LORD, to the house of the God of Jacob; that he may teach us his ways and that we may walk in his paths" (Isaiah 2:3–4; Micah 4:1–4). Israel's spiritual foundations will remain solid while boundaries dramatically expand. In contrast to this inclusive vision, Ezekiel (25–32) features judgment against seven foreign nations.

"BOTH ARE WORDS OF THE LIVING GOD"

Christians do well to learn from ancient Jewish rabbinic debates over boundaries, interpretation of scripture, and tradition. At the time of Jesus there was vigorous debate between followers ("houses") of two leading rabbis in Jerusalem—Shammai and Hillel. Rabbi Shammai was a conservative who adhered to the letter of the law. Rabbi Hillel was more lenient, seeking the spirit of the law. Jewish tradition tells us that these scripture interpreters and their disciples often disagreed on how to apply Jewish law to daily life, as we see in the following account:

> For three years there was a dispute between the House of Shammai and the House of Hillel, the former asserting [that] the law is in accordance with our views, and the latter contending [that] the law is in accordance with our views. Then a heavenly voice went forth and said, "Both are the words of the living God, but the law is in accordance with the rulings of the House of Hillel."
>
> Since, however, both are the words of the living God, what was it that entitled the House of Hillel to have the law decided in accordance with their rulings? Because they were kindly and modest, they studied their own rulings and those of the House of Shammai, and not only that, but even mentioned the opinions of the House of Shammai before their own. (Babylonian Talmud, *Eruvin* 13b)

Authors of this account recognized that people on *both* sides of a theological debate can be right, can both speak "words of the living God." Followers of Hillel so valued their opponents that they quoted opinions of Shammaites before their own.

Another ancient story about the two great rabbis shows their contrasting ways of dealing with outsiders to the faith community. It involves a Gentile who

> wanted to convert to Judaism. This happened not infrequently, and this individual stated that he would accept Judaism only if a rabbi would teach him the entire Torah while he, the prospective convert, stood on one foot. First he went to Shammai, who, insulted by this ridiculous request, threw him out of the house. The man did not give up and went to Hillel. This gentle sage accepted the challenge, and said: "What is hateful to you, do not do to your neighbor. That is the whole Torah; the rest is the explanation of this—go and study it." (Babylonian Talmud, *Shabbat* 31)[4]

I love this story because Hillel's spirit and teaching remind me of Jesus. He could also teach the essence of the law while an inquirer stood, so to speak, on one foot (see, for example, Matthew 22:34–40).

In about AD 200, Jewish scholars began compiling oral traditions of Hillel and Shammai and other rabbis into a written text called the Mishnah ("repetition"). Centuries later the Mishnah became the core of the 2.5-million-word Talmud ("learning" or "study"). Rabbis featured in the Talmud often strongly disagree with each other. Topics debated include Bible interpretation, customs, ethics, purity regulations, folklore, and much more. "Instead of feeling constrained to make a judgment about which argument was correct," writes New

Testament scholar Loren Johns, "the rabbis showed more concern with the importance of thoroughly understanding both sides, often allowing matters to go unresolved."[5]

WE CAN LEARN FROM THE SPIRIT OF RABBI HILLEL

When individuals or groups are in a dispute, they can build trust by respectfully summarizing convictions of opponents in their presence. People in conflict want to at least be heard, not dismissed or ignored. Hillelites were "kindly and modest" in such exchanges, and their interpretations of the Torah prevailed to become the core of mainstream Judaism to this day. How would church and society be different if we had more of the spirit of Hillel?

Early followers of Jesus benefited from the more tolerant spirit of the Hillel rabbinic school. When members of the Sanhedrin at Jerusalem wanted to kill Peter and John, Rabbi Gamaliel—grandson of Hillel—spoke up and said, "Keep away from these men and let them alone; because if this plan or this undertaking is of human origin, it will fail; but if it is of God, you will not be able to overthrow them—in that case you may even be found fighting against God!" (Acts 5:38–39).

Later, Paul tells the Sanhedrin that he was brought up "at the feet of Gamaliel, educated strictly according to our ancestral law" (Acts 22:3). Paul's early ardor for persecuting Christians suggests that he indeed was "educated strictly," taught by Gamaliel but drawn to the comparatively rigid theology of Shammai. After experiencing the grace of God in Jesus Christ, the apostle seems—like Jesus himself—to resonate with the spirit of Hillel.

Chapter 2
REFLECT AND DISCUSS

1. What boundary practices or debates have you experienced in family, church, or nation? If these caused tension, how was that resolved?

2. Ezra and Ruth seem to represent contrasting perspectives on boundaries of a community, and both are in the Bible. Can you think of other surprising contrasts in the Bible regarding wealth, violence, marriage, suffering, or other matters?

3. If the church is going to accept diversity today, do we need a strong center, clear boundaries, or both?

4. What questions does this chapter raise for you?

3

JESUS ALSO LIVED *in a* POLARIZED SOCIETY

Imagine Jesus standing at the back of a raucous town meeting hall in the United States. Angry speakers take the floor to decry gun violence, blaming permissive laws and greedy arms dealers. Equally agitated persons warn that big government will take away their means of self-protection. Someone quotes the Second Amendment that gives them the right to bear arms. On everyone's mind are images of recent mass killings.

What does Jesus do? I doubt that he yells slogans or storms to the microphone. I believe he weeps as he did when he looked over polarized Jerusalem and said, "If you, even you, had only recognized on this day the things that make for peace! But now they are hidden from your eyes" (Luke 19:42). Jesus did not avoid conflict or hesitate to confront injustice but did so with relationship-building love.

STORM CLOUDS WERE ON THE HORIZON IN JESUS' DAY

The American Civil War, in which slavery was a bitterly polarizing issue, began in 1861 and unleashed massive bloodshed. While armies marching into battle Gettysburg-style will not happen today, half of Americans said in a recent poll that they expect a civil war in the United States in the next few years.[1]

That was the danger in Palestine when Jesus wept over Jerusalem. The divisive issue was not slavery, but how Jews should respond to the Roman Empire and its henchmen who had a firm grip on Palestine. Rome had occupied Palestine for a century, and Jews disagreed on how to deal with their overlords.

A generation after Jesus' ministry, tensions among Jews and tensions with Rome exploded into a bloody revolt. Looking out over Jerusalem on his last trip to the city, Jesus said, "The days will come upon you, when your enemies will set up ramparts around you and surround you. . . . They will crush you to the ground, . . . and they will not leave within you one stone upon another" (Luke 19:43–44).

That is exactly what happened. Rome mercilessly crushed the Jewish Revolt of AD 66–70 and crucified so many captives that they "ran out of wood for crosses, and room for crosses even if they had found more wood."[2] Today at one end of the Western Wall[3] in Jerusalem there is still a heap of colossal building stones that Roman soldiers hurled down when they destroyed the temple. The victors sold thousands of Jews into slavery, and the holy city lay in ruins.

A SERIES OF FOREIGN EMPIRES TRAUMATIZED GOD'S PEOPLE

Jewish history shows the growing polarization that led up to this catastrophe. Jews started coming back from Babylonian exile in 538 BC with hopes of recovering something of the glory of the King David era. Grief for all that was lost in exile blended with cautious hope for freedom under their new overlords, the Persians. When returnees built a modest temple where Solomon's had stood, worshipers shouted praise to God and old people wept (Ezra 3:10–13).

Return from exile did not bring much glory. Instead, Judea after the exile was something like countries of eastern Europe that got jerked around in shifting alliances and conflicts between Russia, Germany, England, and the United States during and after World War II. In generations between the Old and New Testaments, the small nation of Judea endured almost constant foreign rule—a cascading catastrophe for God's people.

Centuries earlier, during King David's reign, great regional powers of Egypt and Mesopotamia (modern-day Iraq) were preoccupied with internal problems. But the big cats eventually got their act together, then pounced. Assyria devoured the northern kingdom (Israel) in 722 BC, and Babylon seized the southern kingdom (Judah) in 586 BC and took the final wave of Jewish people into exile. Then, as described in the previous chapter, Persia (modern-day Iran) promptly defeated Babylon, and the unexpected happened: Persia allowed Jews to return to their homeland but granted them only limited self-rule.

Greece was the next predatory empire. Daniel 8 portrays not a cat, but a goat (Greece) charging into a ram (Persia). The goat "threw the ram down to the ground and trampled upon it." That goat was Alexander the Great, who defeated Persia in 331 BC. Alexander then came through Palestine on his way to Egypt, and Jerusalem surrendered without a fight.[4]

But Alexander soon died, and his successors with their Greek culture ruled Palestine for the next century and a half. Jews successfully rebelled in 167 BC,[5] but their independence did not turn out well. Jewish fighters who threw off the foreign yoke were corrupt and ruled the nation poorly. The situation spiraled into civil war, and Rome intervened in 63 BC.

Throughout the New Testament era and far beyond, Rome controlled the entire Mediterranean world. Rome was proud of having brought the Pax Romana (Roman peace), but it was more pacification than peace.

JEWS SPLINTER INTO FACTIONS IN RESPONSE TO FOREIGN RULE

Rome took care of cooperative elites in lands they conquered, giving them business opportunities or administrative posts, and bringing their children to Rome for education. Herod the Great, for example, received his royal crown not in Jerusalem but in Italy by action of the Roman senate. Provincial elites benefited from alliance with Rome, but common people paid high taxes, carried heavy packs for Roman soldiers, and learned that resistance ended in crucifixion. Rome looked so powerful that many of its subjects across the Mediterranean world treated the emperor as divine. This offended devout Jews, who insisted that only God was worthy of worship.

Given the intense religious and political forces that roiled Palestine, it's not surprising that polarized Jews splintered into factions. Gospel accounts and other sources name the following:

1. *Herodians: supported Herod and tried to get along with Rome*

   Herodians were Jews who supported Herod and his dynasty. Herod was only half Jewish and, like his father who was assassinated, collaborated with Rome. Even while lavishly rebuilding the temple to Yahweh in Jerusalem, Herod was constructing temples for emperor worship at Caesarea, Samaria, and Banias—all within Jewish territory.

2. *Sadducees: administered the temple but accommodated Rome*

   Sadducees were aristocratic priests who controlled the Jerusalem temple and tried to keep good relations with Rome. They offered a daily sacrifice for the emperor's well-being, funded by the imperial household. Sadducees supervised religious festivals, including Passover. They were the dominant party in the Sanhedrin, the religious governing body of the Jews.

3. *Pharisees: focused on obeying the Torah and oral tradition*

   Pharisees were lay scholars and religious law experts. They controlled the synagogues, immersing themselves in the Hebrew Bible and the vast Oral Torah with its countless applications. They memorized these traditional interpretations and recounted rabbinic debates about Sabbath regulations, dietary laws, agricultural practices, and much more. Pharisees tithed, obeyed purity laws, honored the Sabbath, and admonished others to do the same.

4. *Essenes: withdrew into ritually pure community and apocalyptic expectation*

   These Torah-reading separatists viewed Jews who controlled the Jerusalem temple as agents of darkness in unholy alliance with Rome. Some Essenes withdrew into a monastery-like community at Qumran in the desert where they wrote or collected the Dead Sea Scrolls that were rediscovered in the twentieth century. Those scrolls contain Old Testament books, commentaries on those scriptures, and apocalyptic texts that anticipate imminent arrival of the kingdom of God and judgment on Rome.

5. *Zealots: took up weapons against Romans and their Jewish collaborators*

Revolutionaries and nationalists, Zealots were ready to use violence and terror to oust Rome and its Jewish collaborators. Some waged guerrilla-style attacks or championed messianic deliverers. Even before full-scale war against Rome erupted in AD 66, Roman soldiers crucified thousands of Jewish men who participated in failed resistance movements.

There was overlap and interaction between these groups. Sadducees, for example, who administered the temple and tried to appease Rome, presumably were sympathetic with Herodians who supported the empire's closest allies in Judea, the Herod family. Pharisees sometimes teamed up with Sadducees or Herodians to try to get Jesus into trouble.

NORTH AMERICAN CHRISTIANS ARE DIVIDED INTO FACTIONS

There are no direct parallels between factions of ancient Jewish society and groupings in the North American church today, but in both eras we see factions jostling for influence. In the United States, for example, you likely will recognize the following categories today even if you might label them differently:

- *Christian nationalists*, who believe that the United States is an inherently Christian nation. These people hold that the American founding fathers were godly men who knew the Bible and wrote a divinely inspired constitution. Public schools should feature laudable aspects of American history without much attention to slavery or the suffering of Native peoples. Government should protect individual freedoms, especially the right to bear arms. Christians should stand for the national anthem, serve in the military when needed, support capital punishment, and oppose abortion.

- *Christian social activists*, whose mission includes seeking justice for minority groups such as Black people, Native Americans, immigrants, and LGBTQ persons. Women deserve equal economic opportunity and reproductive rights. Workers need a living wage, and all Americans should have affordable healthcare. Guns are a scourge, climate change demands urgent action, and Black lives matter. American history lessons should include attention to injustice inflicted upon minorities.

- *Family values Christians*, who lament what they see as an erosion of traditional moral standards and priorities. The Bible is without error and teaches that marriage or sexual intimacy between persons of the same gender is sin. Support for transgender individuals is wrong, and feminism threatens family structures that God established. Home schooling and private schools can most reliably teach children traditional marriage, chastity, patriotism, and literal interpretation of the Bible.

- *Mission conservatives*, who believe that eternal salvation for individuals can only come through Jesus, who gave his life as atonement for sin. Mission is primarily about inviting others to confess faith in Jesus. Since humankind and the entire cosmos will degrade until Christ returns to bring the kingdom of God, Christians do not make social or environmental justice a high priority. Believers can relate respectfully to persons of other religions, but we will not see them in heaven.

- *Mission liberals*, who believe that salvation is more about working for justice now than about where we go when we die. Jesus faced state execution because he confronted powers of oppression, greed, and violence. Mission is primarily about taking up the struggle for a fair society, peace between nations, and a healthy environment. Evangelism means enlisting others to join the quest for justice. It is just as important to follow the example and teaching of Jesus as to worship him as cosmic Lord.

People within these groups will disagree with members of other groups on what they prioritize, though at times their priorities might align or overlap. But generally speaking, they will have diverging views on the Bible, the role of government, the use of violence, the meaning of salvation, and more. Deepening such differences within the church is the increasing political and social polarization of American society.

JESUS CONSTANTLY REACHED ACROSS FACTIONAL BOUNDARIES

Jesus also lived in a polarized society and repeatedly reached across major fault lines separating factions. His followers came from varying political and religious factions, and out of this mix Jesus created community. Not many Christians in the United States and Canada today will try to build spiritual bonds with people whose political or social values we find repugnant. But in our employment, community projects, families, and even congregational activities we often find ourselves alongside persons who do not seem like kindred spirits. The way that Jesus reached across political and spiritual chasms can inspire us to build productive relationships.

Jesus and the Herodians

Consider how Jesus related to persons who were lackeys of Rome. Gospel writers do not label anyone in Jesus' inner circle as a "Herodian," but some of his disciples had collaborated with Herod and the empire. It is startling to see Jesus summon a customs officer to be a disciple, calling Matthew out of his tax booth in Galilee (Matthew 9:9).

This collaborator collected taxes that lined the pockets of the emperor, of Herod, and of the tax collector himself. "Tax farmers" such as Matthew bid a flat amount to hold their office, then enriched themselves by extracting more money than required from fellow Jews. Peasants unable to pay could end up in slavery.[6] Anyone sharing in this scheme would seem an unlikely candidate for Jesus' justice-oriented agenda.

But something about Jesus' manner and teaching attracted even collaborators such as Matthew. Immediately after calling him, Jesus shared a meal with "tax collectors and sinners" (see Matthew 9:10–13). Mention of these two groups in one phrase suggests they were equally dubious people. In this case, "sinners" were probably not the poor and oppressed, but the rich and powerful.

Pharisees watching Jesus were scandalized and demanded to know why he was at table with collaborators and other suspect characters. But Jesus persisted in hanging out with despised individuals. Passing through Jericho on his way to Jerusalem, Jesus spotted chief tax collector Zacchaeus watching the procession from his perch in a sycamore tree. "Hurry and come down," Jesus said, "I must stay at your house today." Those were presumably kind words because Zacchaeus welcomed Jesus into his home (see Luke 19:1–10).

Jesus may have hung out with corrupt people, but he did not hesitate to confront their wrongdoing. While Jesus was his guest, Zacchaeus admitted that he had been dishonest in collecting taxes. "Half of my possessions . . . I will give to the poor," he promised, "and if I have defrauded anyone, . . . I will pay back four times as much."

In contrast to some tax collectors who befriended Jesus, other Herodians plotted to destroy him and set a trap (Mark 3:6; Matthew 22:15–22). They tried to corner him with a question: Is it acceptable under Jewish law to pay taxes to the emperor? Say yes, and Jesus could lose support among Jews who chafed under Roman rule. Say no, and Herod might lock up or kill Jesus as he had John the Baptist.

Jesus knew that he would die in Jerusalem at the hands of corrupt powerbrokers but did not lash out in hatred. "Go and tell that fox for me," Jesus said of Herod, "'I am casting out demons and performing cures today and tomorrow, and on the third day I finish my work'" (Luke 13:32). Instead of responding with threats of his own, Jesus carried on with the work God had given him.

Matthew and Zacchaeus likely abandoned their empire-serving careers when they followed Jesus. But Jesus often related respectfully even toward people whose political agenda ran counter to the kingdom of God. Would I have patience to build such relationships with persons aligned with nationalism or with business interests that I think are corrupt?

Jesus and the Sadducees

Jesus had substantial theological and class differences with the aristocratic priests who managed the Jerusalem temple. Belief in resurrection at the last judgment, held by many Jews in the first century, became a central theme for Jesus and his followers. Sadducees rejected the idea. In a public exchange, they set Jesus up for ridicule by citing a law from Deuteronomy that says a man whose brother dies without male offspring shall marry the widow to produce an heir (Luke 20:27–44; cf. Deuteronomy 25:5–10).

Suppose a woman is widowed and remarried seven times, said the Sadducees. Whose wife will she be at the end-time resurrection? Can you hear the crowd laughing? Most of us find it difficult to be courteous to someone who ridicules our beliefs, but Luke records Jesus giving a full and thoughtful response. He seems to have related respectfully to Sadducees in such public settings.

Jesus did, however, burn bridges with the Sadducees in an act of civil disobedience at the temple they administered. Jewish pilgrims who came long distances wanted animals for sacrifice and needed to exchange foreign money to make offerings. Entrepreneurs provided for these needs at booths in the temple courtyard, but apparently at rip-off rates. Seeing this, Jesus overturned tables and stopped all traffic. The temple was to be a house of prayer, he declared, "but you have made it a den of robbers" (Mark 11:17).

Mark specifies that Jesus upended the seats of dove sellers (11:15). The dove was a poor person's sacrifice, the most they could afford (Leviticus 5:7). Jesus saw worshipers who were already financially vulnerable being ripped off and was not going to make nice in response. When the chief priests (Sadducees) who administered the temple learned of Jesus' actions, they plotted to kill him. This was a confrontation with corrupt institutional and economic power structures.

The account of Jesus upending tables in the temple (John 2:13–17) does not justify the use of violence against people. Though Jesus improvised a whip for that action, scripture specifies that the whip was for driving out sheep and cattle. The money changers remained, and Jesus spoke sharply to them. Sadducees reacted angrily to this incident. They had pre-occupations typical of institutional leaders: desire for stability and sustainability, caution about innovation, and willingness to accommodate political or economic forces necessary for survival.

Jesus and the Pharisees

Devout students and practitioners of Jewish law, Pharisees largely operated at the grassroots level of Jewish society. They were laymen, teachers, and ordinary businessmen. Jesus had much debate with Pharisees, probably because he was so much like them in being a teacher of the law among common people.

Although the Talmud—a written record of Pharisees' teaching—was not completed until centuries later, it gives us an idea of what they believed at the time of Jesus. Consider the similarity between Jesus' teaching and these phrases from a Talmud document called *Pirkei Avot*, or "Ethics of the Fathers":

- Love peace and pursue peace (*Pirkei Avot* 1:12).
- One who seeks to make his name great destroys it (1:13).
- Do [God's] will as if it were your own (2:4).
- Do not judge your fellow until you have stood in his place (2:4).
- The more possessions, the more worry (2:8).
- Do not be quick to anger (2:15).
- Do not pray as though by rote but plead for mercy and grace before God (2:18).

Pharisees did not have a formal organization, so Jesus was not a "member." Pharisees simply were men who rigorously studied, debated, and professed to live out even the vast Oral Torah. Jesus got impatient with this "tradition of the elders"

(Matthew 15:2), because it sometimes added unnecessary burdens or defeated the main point of scripture.

As commonly happens among religious peers, Jesus and the Pharisees had both friendly encounters and heated debates. He did not hate the Pharisees but hated their hypocrisy. "Do whatever they teach you and follow it," he said, "but do not do as they do, for they do not practice what they teach" (Matthew 23:3). The whole of Matthew 23 is Jesus' scathing indictment of hypocrites—a "brood of vipers."

When a Pharisee named Simon invited Jesus to his home for a meal, word got around. A woman "who was a sinner" (Luke 7:37) entered Simon's courtyard and wept at Jesus' feet while he reclined at the table. Pharisees tried to avoid sinful people, and here the label implies moral compromise. Simon was scandalized. In response, Jesus told the parable of a man—perhaps a stand-in for Simon—who was filled with gratitude because a creditor forgave his massive debt.

Pharisees cultivated a tradition of heated theological exchange among themselves, and Jesus knew how to engage such debates. With Pharisees he debated whether ritual cleansing was necessary before eating (Luke 11:37–54), why one should take the humblest place at a meal (14:7–11), and why the kingdom of God will include the physically disabled and the poor (14:15–24). Such exchanges sometimes got testy.

But Jesus met Pharisees on their own turf and sustained dialogue with them. Some eventually became believers and participated in the Jerusalem Council where the early Christians debated whether Gentiles in the church needed to be circumcised (Acts 15:5). Paul counted himself among the Pharisees (Philippians 3:4–6), and he also engaged in lively debate with his Pharisee peers.

Jesus and the Essenes

Jesus was not an Essene but had things in common with them. The baptism he received from John probably happened not far from the Qumran (Essene) community. Like the radical residents of Qumran, John had pulled away from the corrupt religious establishment at Jerusalem to take up a life of devotion in the desert. Both John and the Essenes condemned spiritual compromise and set out to "prepare the way of the Lord" in the wilderness (Luke 3:4–6; cf. Isaiah 40:3). Both practiced baptism in preparation for the kingdom of God.

Jesus himself had forty days of spiritual testing in the desert. Like the Essenes, he viewed the world in terms of light and darkness ("I am the light of the world," John 8:12) and rejected Jewish leadership in Jerusalem. However, he socialized with persons who suffered disease, sinners who did not observe the Law of Moses, and others whom Essenes avoided. Instead of teaching only an exclusive circle of followers in private as the Essenes did, Jesus preached to thousands of common people in public.

Jesus and the Zealots

Among Jesus' apostles was "Simon, who was called the Zealot" (Luke 6:15).[7] Zealots were Jewish nationalists who fiercely championed the Law of Moses, opposed foreign government in Palestine, and figured significantly in the Jewish Revolt (AD 66–70). Simon the Zealot may have been such an extremist, though we cannot be certain. It is possible that Jesus recruited him out of the violence-prone political movement.

Some Zealots were daggermen, called Sicarii for the short, curved sword (*sica*) they secretly carried to kill. They were terrorists who mingled with crowds at Jewish festivals where they assassinated Roman soldiers and Jewish collaborators. Before

Jesus' disciples headed from the upper room to the garden of Gethsemane where Jesus would be arrested, they told Jesus that they had two swords (Luke 22:35–38).[8] One belonged to Peter, who soon used it to attack the high priest's slave (John 18:10). The other perhaps belonged to Simon the Zealot.

Though Jesus may have interacted with Zealots or even had one among his followers, he rejected their strategy of armed resistance. "Love your enemies and pray for those who persecute you," he taught (Matthew 5:44). Recognizing that war against Rome would soon begin, Jesus told his followers not to fight. When armies surround Jerusalem, he said, "those in Judea must flee to the mountains" (Luke 21:21).

JESUS SHOWS HOW TO BUILD IMPROBABLE RELATIONSHIPS

Jesus befriended and collaborated with people from a breathtaking diversity of political and theological backgrounds. He occasionally rebuked them or argued with them, but he usually maintained relationship. He went beyond critique to invite them to a greater goal: embracing the liberating grace of the kingdom of God. Neither Jesus nor his followers saved the Jewish nation from the harsh polarization that culminated in disastrous war against Rome. Tens of thousands of Jews— including many noncombatants—would die, and the temple would be in ruins.

Our reconciliation efforts alone will not save church or society from fragmentation. Along with heaven's great multitude, we proclaim, "Salvation belongs to our God," not to us (Revelation 7:10). But because God plans to unite all things in Christ, we live into that hope and participate in the work of reconciliation. We model our lives on Jesus, who reached across every divide of society, showing love even to people who wanted to destroy him. When we live in that reconciling way, we begin to see God's will "done on earth as it is in heaven." We can have the joy of discovering shared humanity and sometimes even spiritual kinship with people whom we might otherwise avoid.

Chapter 3
REFLECT AND DISCUSS

1. Give a modern example of damage caused by polarization that reminds you of stones from the destroyed temple still lying today at the Western Wall.

2. Describe a political, ethnic, or religious group today that you think might feel threatened in the way that Jews who returned from Babylonian exile felt threatened by foreign cultures. How does that group define or maintain boundaries?

3. Which of the Jewish factions of Jesus' day is most similar to your way of functioning in church or society? With which factions of Christianity in modern society do you most identify? Are you alienated from some? Why and how?

4. In what ways might the example of Jesus reaching across boundaries of factions inspire you to do the same today? What risks would that involve?

5. What questions does this chapter raise for you?

4

WE ARE LEPERS
in a WORLD THAT
NEEDS HEALING

Would I join a circle of ten men in local leadership who planned to meet monthly to talk about vocation and faith? That invitation came in 2012 from a friend seeking a greater sense of shared mission with others in the local community. The proposed group would include persons with responsibility in government, medicine, psychology, education, business, and church. We would talk about our lives and respect confidentiality.

For more than a decade, that group in Indiana has convened to share stories, encourage one another, and exchange counsel. Overcoming polarization was not a primary reason for convening the group. We are not diverse in gender, socioeconomic status, or sexual orientation. We all are midlife and older. But the circle has always included differences that could have kept us apart. We are Lutheran, Baptist, Mennonite, Catholic, and United Methodist. We are politically liberal, politically conservative, Black, and White. A desire to live faithfully in leadership roles and, in the words of Jeremiah, "seek the welfare of the city" where God placed us (Jeremiah 29:7) drew the group together.

Early on we each took a session to recount our vocational and faith journey. We read books on spirituality, and each had opportunity to speak about what gives our lives purpose. When one participant left the area and nine remained, someone recalled the story of Jesus healing ten lepers. When only one returned to thank him, Jesus asked, *Where are the other nine?* Given that all of us at some point shared about wounding in our lives, we started to call our group the Lepers.

SERVE THE COMMUNITY AND SUPPORT EACH OTHER

Ten years into our project, the Lepers met over breakfast to assess what we have learned. "We have differences of opinion," a theological and political liberal ventured, "but in ten years we've never had destructive arguments." But before we did any more self-congratulation, a political conservative declared that for him the meetings have not always been edifying. "Let's put it right out on the table . . . Trump."

With most members of the group leaning toward the theological and political left, it had been easy for us to insert digs about the recent American president. "I never particularly liked the man with orange hair," the conservative allowed. "But I thought that some of his policies were good for the country." The Lepers had unproductively focused on a politician's personality without really engaging issues that attracted people to him.

So why does someone with such sympathies stay in the conversation? This Leper cited Benjamin Franklin, who helped found the American Philosophical Society. The organization today retains its mission of "promoting useful knowledge" in science, technology, and the humanities for the good of wider society.[1] "Franklin wanted creative people to put aside personal interests and work together for common goals," our friend said. "This group appealed to me for the same reason."

THINK LIKE SCIENTISTS IN SEARCH OF TRUTH

"I want to be like a scientist focused on inquiry and curiosity," another Leper added. Even in the current polarized political environment, he said, "if you listen well, you learn that there is a huge overlap between what Republicans and Democrats want: good schools for our children, sufficient income, adequate housing, quality medical care, and safe neighborhoods."

He told what happened five years earlier when the federal government wanted to build a twelve-hundred-bed Immigration and Customs Enforcement (ICE) detention center in our county.[2] This political conservative was in local elected office at the time and presided when five hundred people showed up for a town meeting on the issue. He favored accepting the ICE detention center because it would provide both tax income for the region and, he believed, more humane facilities for detainees.

Also pursuing humanitarian goals, local pastors (including me) categorically opposed the new facility. Though we differed on whether to accept the detention center, both this politician and his activist opponents wanted to do what they believed was humane. My memory is that this public official remained calm and listened well in public discussions. But he remembers a time in the detention center dispute when he lost patience.

"It was nine o'clock at the end of a long day, and I was fielding questions at a town meeting," he recalled. "In front of an audience of several hundred, a teenage girl came to the microphone and made an unhelpful statement. I snapped, 'You're wrong!' and shut her down." Memory of that exchange is still painful for this Leper years later. "I needed to listen better," he says.

THE NEW TESTAMENT PROVIDES CONTRASTING MODELS FOR ENGAGING SOCIETY

The Lepers group reflects a cross-section of Christian witness in government, business, education, healthcare, and pastoral care. Each of us could tell stories of polarization and temptation to moral compromise in our areas of work. Lying and disinformation plague our society; abuse of power distorts business, church, and service agencies; greed or arrogance can take root anywhere.

Jesus told his disciples to be "wise as serpents and innocent as doves" (Matthew 10:16) as they found their way in the world. He gave that counsel for followers who were going out into a polarized Jewish society to heal and to cast out unclean spirits. Other parts of the New Testament provide guidance for how followers of Jesus function in a multireligious or pagan world. Below are two New Testament strategies for engaging society that contrast sharply—examples of diversity within scripture.

The apostle Paul: Participate in an idolatrous world but be careful

Paul traveled and wrote his New Testament epistles in the middle of the first century at a time when he could still be cautiously optimistic about the Roman Empire. He wrote all his letters before any Roman emperor killed Christians and before Roman armies destroyed Jerusalem. The apostle claimed and used privileges he enjoyed as a Roman citizen (Acts 22:25).

In his epistle to believers at Rome he said, "Authorities that exist have been instituted by God" (Romans 13:1). When in legal trouble, Paul appealed his case to the emperor's tribunal (Acts 25:10). He earned his living as a tentmaker in Roman-administered cities (Acts 18:1–3; 1 Thessalonians 2:9; 2 Thessalonians 3:7–8) and functioned even within an economy in which many people blasphemously worshiped the emperor as divine. Paul traveled across the Mediterranean on merchant ships that were carrying goods to Rome, the imperial capital (Acts 27:2–6).[3]

The apostle knew that churches at Corinth and Rome had become polarized over *how* to participate in an idolatrous world. One presenting issue was whether it was appropriate for Christians to participate in trade guilds or civic banquets that included emperor worship or food that had been part of pagan rituals ("food offered to idols," see 1 Corinthians 8:1–13; Revelation 2:20–23).

Participation in such activities may have been unavoidable for survival in politics or the business world, so Paul allowed it (Romans 14:1–23). But he acknowledged that some "weak" believers might interpret such participation as compromise and be misled spiritually. Be alert to how your discipleship choices affect fellow Christians, Paul counseled, and "do not let what you eat cause the ruin of one for whom Christ died" (14:15).

The first time I attended a Rotary Club meeting I was taken off guard when everyone stood, turned toward the American flag, and pledged allegiance. I stood but remained silent because allegiance is such a comprehensive commitment that I want to give it to Christ alone. When the pledge was finished, the man beside me said in a friendly tone, "So you're Canadian?" He seemed perplexed when I tried to explain my stance.

Paul said we should not pass judgment on one another on matters such as this (Romans 14:13–14). Though I disagree with Christians who pledge to a flag, I respect them.[4] Elsewhere in the world followers of Jesus face far more difficult choices when engaging societies with military conscription, totalitarian government, religious persecution, or other extreme pressures to conform. Christians in those contexts might find a second New Testament strategy more useful.

John of Patmos: Withdraw from idolatrous structures of society

A generation after Paul wrote letters reflecting his engagement of Roman society, John of Patmos received a vision portraying the Roman Empire as a beast channeling demonic power. In the decades between these two writers, the Roman government sometimes turned against the church. Many Christians, apparently including both Peter and Paul, died as martyrs in Rome after the great fire of AD 64.

The Roman army destroyed Jerusalem in AD 70 and crucified thousands of its defenders. Two late first-century emperors—Nero and Domitian—were especially notorious for cruelty, vanity, and blasphemous preening. Presumably a political exile for resisting such misrule, John simply says he was on the tiny island of Patmos "because of the word of God and the testimony of Jesus" (Revelation 1:9).

Given John's circumstances, it's no surprise that he rejected any involvement with people or institutions associated with the empire. Rome ("the great city that rules over the kings of the earth," Revelation 17:18) had become a harlot, "fornicating" with kings of the earth. John calls the imperial capital "Babylon," which destroyed Solomon's temple in 586 BC just like Rome destroyed the Jewish temple in AD 70. Fueling John's fury was the increasing practice of emperor worship. Participating in a parade to honor the "divine" emperor or offering a sacrifice to his image apparently eased access to business, political, and social circles. John said *no way*.

Though he names only one Christian martyr in Revelation, John expected there would be more (2:13; 6:9–11). He condemns all who collaborate with Roman institutions as worshipers of the beast. Any who would "eat food sacrificed to idols" he calls "Balaam" or "Jezebel" (2:14; 2:20–23). Rome with its powerful tentacles was about to fall, and Christians must break all ties while they could. "Come out of her," he says, "so that you do not take part in her sins" (18:4).

There is much for North American Christians to learn from John's vision about how government and society can become idolatrous. In the United States, our nation's perversions of power have resulted in slavery, slaughter of Indigenous people, invasion of foreign nations, systemic racism, and illicit blending of church and state. But Revelation especially is relevant to societies where government morphs in extreme ways beyond its God-given role as servant for the common good (Romans 13:1–7).

In their 1934 Theological Declaration of Barmen, Christian resisters to Hitler's blasphemies called fellow believers back to their confessional roots. "We reject the false doctrine that there could be areas of our life in which we would not belong to Jesus Christ but to other lords," they declared. The church must never cede ultimate authority to the state or to one persuasive human. Nor can the church simply be an arm of government. The Barmen authors wrote, "We reject the false doctrine that beyond its special commission the Church should and could take on the nature, tasks, and dignity which belong to the State and thus become itself an organ of the State."[5]

THE NEW JERUSALEM IS A MODEL FOR HOW THE
CHURCH FUNCTIONS

Although the book of Revelation addresses Christians living
in extreme circumstances, it also presents a positive picture
of Christian community. Rome had destroyed the earthly city
of Jerusalem in AD 70, but now John sees a *New* Jerusalem
"coming down out of heaven from God, prepared as a bride
adorned for her husband" (Revelation 21:2). This is a present,
emerging reality for John, not just a dream of the future. It is
an embodiment of the Lord's Prayer, "Your will be done on
earth as it is in heaven."

Early chapters of Revelation portray the throne room of
heaven, where a community worships God and the Lamb.
Now the church on earth becomes a tangible expression of
that healing reality. John's New Jerusalem imagery (especially
Revelation 4–7, 21–22) suggests the following for how the
church can operate in a fallen and polarized world:

*1. God's people focus more on what is at the center of the
community than on what makes us different.* The triune God
(Creator, Lamb, Spirit) is the focal point of allegiance in both
heaven and earth (Revelation 4–6). Worship unites people of
every nation, tribe, and language. Worshipers do not themselves resolve all problems of the world but rejoice that "salvation belongs to our God" (see 7:9–17).

*2. The faith community has boundaries but does not shut
out people.* The New Jerusalem has walls—moral, political,
economic, and social boundaries—beyond which followers
of the Lamb do not go. Outside the walls are "dogs and
sorcerers and fornicators and murderers and idolaters, and
everyone who loves and practices falsehood" (22:15).[6] Dehu-
manizing practices of spiritual manipulation, lust, violence,
and deceit that occur in corrupt regions of society have no

place in the church. But gates of the faith community always remain open (21:25).

3. *The faith community has no elitism, racism, or economic inequality.* The New Jerusalem is enormous, measuring twelve thousand stadia (1,500 miles) in length, width, *and height* (see 21:15–21). It is thousands of times bigger than Rome, and all territory of the Roman Empire could fit within its limits. The New Jerusalem features precious jewels for all to enjoy, and everyone walks on streets of gold. Kings enter with their splendor, and people of countless cultures bring in the "honor of the nations" (see 21:24–26).

4. *God's gracious presence makes this community a place of restoration.* From the throne flows water of life that nurtures abundant fruit trees and brings healing to the nations. Structures of society return to their God-ordained places. Loud voices in heaven proclaim, "The kingdom of the world has become the kingdom of our Lord . . . and he will reign forever and ever" (11:15). Far from depicting destruction of planet Earth, Revelation envisions glorious renewal. That hope sustains followers of Jesus.

THE KINGDOM OF GOD IS "ALREADY BUT NOT YET"

It is risky to derive too much specific application for how the church should function from such symbolic imagery. But major contours of the redeemed community seem clear. The faith community is not an exclusive or homogenous club, but a gift from God that includes surprising people—eventually even kings of the earth who were villains of earlier chapters in Revelation (18:3; 21:24). Polarities are no longer destructive where God and the Lamb reign in love.

We call Christ *Lord* in a world that does not recognize his sovereignty, and we see this tension in Hebrews 2:5–9. The writer asserts that, in Jesus, God fulfilled the divine intent to "[put] everything in subjection" (2:8 ESV) under the feet of the "son of man" (see Psalm 8:3–8 ESV). Hebrews 2 takes the son of man in Psalm 8 to be Jesus. The author acknowledges that "at present, we do not yet see everything in subjection to" him. "But we see . . . Jesus," who as promised in Psalm 8, is "crowned with glory and honor because of the suffering of death" (Hebrews 2:8–9 ESV).[7]

With eyes on Jesus, Christians claim citizenship in the new social and political order that he inaugurated and live as resident aliens in the world.[8] The kingdom of God "has come near" (Matthew 4:17), Jesus told his disciples, and "is among you" (Luke 17:21). Followers of Jesus *already* aspire to live by the Sermon on the Mount and other New Testament expressions of the emerging kingdom. To sustain such countercultural lives in a fractured world, we need the power of the Holy Spirit and the support of a worshiping community. Solidarity we find in the church will not end polarization even within the faith community but will help us deal with differences in healthy ways.

WE CAN LEARN FROM POLARITIES IN THE NEW TESTAMENT

The stark contrast between the apostle Paul and John of Patmos in their response to the Roman government can help us understand why Christians today end up with contrasting theological or ethical understandings. Paul and John found themselves in very different circumstances, and that shaped their theology. We find other polarities within the New Testament, such as early Christian teaching on the role of women in church leadership. Paul tells believers at Corinth, "Women should be silent in the churches. For they are not permitted to speak, but should be subordinate, as the law also says. If there is anything they desire to know, let them ask their husbands at home" (1 Corinthians 14:34–35).[9]

But Paul then goes on to counsel women at Corinth to wear a veil *when* they pray or prophesy—apparently in public worship.[10] He praises Phoebe, a leader of the church at Cenchreae, who evidently delivered the book of Romans to Italy (Romans 16:1–2). Prisca (Priscilla) and Aquila were a wife and husband teaching team who collaborated with Paul (Romans 16:3–5; Acts 18:26).

Limitations that some New Testament passages place on women in church seem to reflect circumstances of specific contexts. Most Jewish men coming into the church had spent years or decades learning the Torah. They were far more likely than women to have in-depth theological background, so Paul directed women who became Christian to "learn in silence with full submission" (1 Timothy 2:11). But when women acquired adequate tools, Paul apparently was ready to see them in leadership.

We could find similar diversity in the New Testament regarding speaking in tongues, fasting, divorce, attitudes toward the Law of Moses, and more. When interpreting the Bible and applying it to our lives, we are wise to examine the context behind a given teaching and appreciate the tension that exists *within* the Bible on the subject. If modern readers of the Bible come to contrasting interpretations, those might reflect their differing circumstances.

COUNTERPOINT IN THE BIBLE IS A GIFT

Do not be disheartened by diversity in scripture; it is a gift. God created us in the divine image, making us stewards and co-creators, and granting us options. Scripture displays the breadth of ways the Spirit of God has moved in diverse faith communities and in previous generations. Writing to believers at Corinth, Paul says, "We are God's fellow workers" (1 Corinthians 3:9 ESV).[11] Since humans with all our variations are co-creators, churches we build will not all look alike.

The nonnegotiable is that Jesus Christ be the foundation. Paul says church leaders variously build on that foundation with gold, silver, precious stones, wood, hay, or straw. Judgment day will reveal the integrity of each choice. Though some structures will go up in smoke, "the builder will be saved, but only as through fire" (see 1 Corinthians 3:10–15).

Aware that the church at Corinth was prone to destructive factionalism (1 Corinthians 3:3–4), Paul underscored the importance of unity. "Do you not know that you [plural] are God's temple and that God's Spirit dwells in you?" he asks. "If anyone destroys God's temple, God will destroy that person" (3:16–17). Dividing the church is more grievous to God than making some poor choices in exactly how we build the church.

MUST WE DECIDE WHO IS IN AND WHO IS OUT?

Individuals, congregations, and denominations appropriately clarify what we believe on many topics but should be cautious about condemning those who come to different conclusions. "Do not judge, so that you may not be judged," Jesus directed (Matthew 7:1). Jesus would not even condemn the woman taken in adultery (John 8:1–11), and at the Last Supper he broke bread with Judas, who was plotting betrayal (Matthew 26:20–30).

Jesus taught forbearance in his parable of a farmer's field where wheat and weeds grow together (Matthew 13:24–30, 36–43). Laborers want to take out the weeds, but the boss tells them to let both grow together until harvest, when reapers will burn the weeds and keep the grain. The kingdom of heaven may be compared to this, Jesus said. Followers of Jesus should not try to separate the wicked from the righteous, since that will happen "at the end of the age." Jesus appears to have used this laissez-faire image to describe how his followers should function *in the world*, not in the church.[12]

In extreme circumstance, the apostle Paul says, a congregation must shut out an individual who sins and does not repent (1 Corinthians 5:1–13). Likewise, in the book of Revelation, Christ rebukes congregations for tolerating heresy promoted by members whom he disparages as "Balaam" and "Jezebel" (2:14, 20–23). But Christ himself will be the one intervening to stop the sinful individuals. Similarly, it is Christ who will remove a sinful congregation's "lampstand" (2:4–5), not other congregations.

Even this brief discussion of boundaries reveals polarities and ambiguities in the New Testament on matters of church discipline and how we engage the world. We often are wise not to simply cite a single passage and say that settles the matter. We best decide ethical and moral matters in light of the entire witness of scripture. When holding one another accountable, Christians appropriately operate within the polarity between grace and inflexibility. That tension between tolerance and severity warrants careful discernment, and virtually guarantees that faith communities will come out at different places on the continuum.

Chapter 4
REFLECT AND DISCUSS

1. Have you been part of a group that continued to meet despite having considerable theological or political differences? What drew the group together? What pushed you apart? How did you learn from that encounter?

2. Do you find yourself being more of a "scientist" focused on inquiry or a "preacher" proclaiming truth as you see it? Which do you want others around you to be? How does your approach affect your attitude and behavior?

3. How far should Christians go to engage potentially idolatrous institutions or structures of society? What about the military? Political parties or rallies? Wall Street? The entertainment industry? Sports? Service clubs? Church institutions? Educational institutions? Entrepreneurial business?

4. What fresh insights does the description of the New Jerusalem give you? How could these insights affect how the church functions?

5. What questions does this chapter raise for you?

WHY JESUS *and* NICODEMUS TALKED *in the* DARK

Diplomats and conflict mediators sometimes speak of "track two" diplomacy. This differs from "track one" diplomacy, which happens, for example, when heads of state meet to discuss their relationship and seek common ground. Such negotiations happen through official government channels and may result in formal agreements.

Track two diplomacy, in contrast, is informal and unofficial, conducted by nongovernment actors who build relationships and explore possible avenues of understanding or collaboration. Participants in track two diplomacy could be educators, scientists, businesspeople, clergy, or persons of other vocation. The track two process does not have to be secret, but it likely will not occur in the glare of publicity. People who want to get beyond polarization in church or society can take part in such exchanges even on the smallest scale.

RABBI RENDEZVOUS ON A DARK NIGHT

Jesus and Nicodemus would have scratched their beards at "track two" language, but they engaged in something similar when they met on a dark night (John 3:1–21). The kingdom of God movement that Jesus heralded may have featured love, but it had a polarizing effect on parts of Jewish society. A subversive-sounding preacher like Jesus could start a movement that might get the whole Jewish nation into trouble with Rome, and authorities eventually stopped him.[1] But a Pharisee named Nicodemus, a member of the Sanhedrin, risked his standing in Jewish society to seek out Jesus and open a track two conversation. As a "leader of the Jews" (3:1), Nicodemus had access to power circles where steps to deal with Jesus would be taken.

I honor the courage that brought Nicodemus out at night for off-the-record conversation with a Galilean carpenter. I doubt there was anything snarky in his opening words to Jesus, "Rabbi, we know that you are a teacher who has come from God" (3:2). This Pharisee appears to have come with genuine respect and curiosity, and Jesus responded by summarizing the spiritual core of his own message: "No one can see the kingdom of God without being born from above."

When Jesus expanded on that, Nicodemus was bewildered: "How can these things be?" he asked (3:9). A gentle rebuke followed. "Are you a teacher of Israel, and yet you do not understand these things?" (3:10).[2] Those words must have been spoken kindly because Jesus immediately added, "God so loved the world that he gave his only Son . . ." (3:16). Jesus exuded compassion, and Nicodemus felt it. There is little indication that Nicodemus was "born from above" that night. But a personal encounter with the Galilean teacher whom peers of Nicodemus feared or despised changed him.

We see evidence of that change later when Nicodemus defended Jesus when he was in danger during the Festival of Booths in Jerusalem (John 7:50–52). By that time Jesus' reputation was so polarizing that some Jews wanted to kill him, and others thought he was the Messiah (5:18; 7:1, 19, 20, 25, 41). Chief priests and Pharisees sent temple police to arrest Jesus but abandoned the plan because multitudes were mesmerized by his teaching. Such crowds could riot, and the situation became tense as listeners divided into pro-Jesus and anti-Jesus sentiments.

PHARISEES WANT THE AUTHORITIES TO MUZZLE JESUS

Pharisees were the group who had the most frequent clashes with Jesus, and a clutch of them convened at the temple to speak their mind to Jewish religious leaders. Confronting the temple police who had failed to apprehend Jesus, they demanded to know why. Maybe the police themselves had been deceived by that teacher who fooled the ignorant masses, they sarcastically suggested.

Who should speak up at that moment to defend Jesus but Nicodemus! "Our law does not judge people without first giving them a hearing to find out what they are doing, does it?" he inquired (John 7:51). Nicodemus did not attack the temple authorities but asked a question that should have called them back to their own best practices. Instead, they sneered at him. But the fact that Nicodemus, amid skeptical peers, advocated for Jesus suggests that track two diplomacy between Jesus and this leader of the Jews had borne fruit. Even more surprising, Nicodemus showed up with embalming spices to help prepare the body of Jesus for burial after Jesus was executed for insubordination and blasphemy (John 19:39).

GROWLING PICKUPS MIGHT SIGNAL WHITE SUPREMACY

Our young next-door neighbor likes guns and drives a growling pickup with a large American flag that streams in the wind. That might be garden-variety love of country by a White man, but it could also be something more sinister. A flagged pickup does not scare me personally, but how might it feel to an undocumented immigrant or a Black person?

Cyneatha Millsaps, pastor at my home congregation, tells of a flagged truck experience she had at a nearby state park. Pastor Millsaps, who is Black, went to the park alone one day to check out facilities because she was scheduled to speak there soon for a church gathering. As she prepared to leave, a small convoy of pickup trucks streamed in. At least one had an American flag streaming in the wind. "I began wondering about who uses the park and how would they feel about me being there," she writes.

> I know my fear and anxiety are irrational, but they have deep roots. My fears about being harmed in rural areas of our country come from a history of lynching and torture of black bodies who found themselves in the wrong place at the wrong time. African Americans have learned over the centuries that we are not welcomed in many spaces. That our very presence in some areas invites a hatred that is deeply embedded in racism. Our community has internalized those traumas associated with that history and we find it hard to shake. This is what led to my experience of fear even when there was no immediate threat.[3]

All that triggered by a flag on a pickup truck? Yes, symbolic actions can communicate volumes, and my pastor had reason to be frightened. She got out of the state park without incident, but the explanation for her fear is instructive.

The Black community in the United States has endured centuries of violation ranging from outright slavery to Jim Crow laws to lynching and murder. Men driving flagged pickups too often have appeared at rallies and protests promoting racist ideology. Not long ago a Black man jogging through a mostly White neighborhood in Georgia was hunted down and murdered by White men in pickup trucks.[4] The killers made themselves known to police, but there were no arrests for months.

NEIGHBORLY KINDNESS BUILDS TRUST

I reject some values that I see in my neighbor or infer from his flagged pickup. But when a windstorm blew down a tree at our home onto the public roadway, he showed up with a chainsaw before I even got to the scene. Chainsaw track two diplomacy? I doubt he thought of it that way, but I welcomed the initiative and was glad for the opportunity for us to learn to know each other.

A church planter told me that one of the best ways to build trust with neighbors is to let them do something for you. If this evangelist needed a tool such as a garden rake, he sometimes asked to borrow it from a neighbor he did not know. If the neighbor agreed—as usually happened—a relationship could start with the neighbor in the role of helper. The door was then open for the church planter to return the favor to the neighbor. Our neighbor showed his chainsaw kindness even though my wife and I had an immigrant-friendly sign on our lawn that says in Spanish, English, and Arabic, "No matter where you are from, we're glad you're our neighbor." That, too, is a powerful symbolic gesture that surely raises associations in the mind of our neighbor.

He is a blue-collar man with a high school diploma who is learning truck mechanics. I am a white-collar man with advanced degrees who spends a lot of time in meetings and at the computer. Our pickup-driving neighbor might have reason to be uneasy about our immigrant-friendly yard sign. It can be difficult for persons like me to understand why there is resentment about immigration among some blue-collar Americans, or why many are drawn to a strain of conservative politics that seems bigoted to me.

Journalist Steven Greenhouse recently interviewed Rust Belt union members to ask how the media is doing in covering working-class issues. In a typical comment, one steelworker said, "The American worker has been put on the back burner" by the media. Greenhouse reports,

> Several workers said they wanted more local coverage of plant closings, the negative effects of trade, and the waves of layoffs that have hit their communities. Some said they wanted more stories on the difficulties their children face affording college and on the financial challenges of retirement—that is, if they can afford to retire.[5]

What is neglected in much American media is happening in many sectors of American society: industrial workers and those with less formal education feel marginalized, underpaid, and forgotten. Greenhouse notes that "at many news organizations, editors are assigning more 'upscale minded' stories about skiing vacations in Aspen and whether to invest in Apple and fewer pieces about factory closings in Akron and layoffs in Cincinnati."

BACKGROUND AND SOCIAL LOCATION SHAPE PREJUDICES

It seems natural for my wife Ellen and me to welcome immigrants to our city and our church, and it is easiest for us when they are from Latin America. Ellen was raised in Puerto Rico as the daughter of a service-minded surgeon father and an artist-musician mother. I was raised on a farm in Pennsylvania where my father hired Puerto Rican migrant workers. He treated these seasonal employees with respect, but later in life expressed regret for not having given them better lodging while they labored on our farm. His regret helped shape my attitudes toward immigrants and migrant workers.

Ellen and I have had privileges of extensive cross-cultural experience that relatively few Americans enjoy. Ellen is a physical therapist who grew up bilingual, and I am a pastor/academic who learned Spanish by studying in Costa Rica and Spain during college. Neither of us ever felt social or vocational competition from immigrants entering our community. We always had employment for which we were trained and were able to save for retirement.

I don't know if my flag-flying neighbor senses competition from recent immigrants for jobs he wants, but many workers today feel themselves losing ground on multiple fronts. Blue-collar jobs have been outsourced to foreign countries or replaced by technology. Immigrants are sometimes willing to take lower-paying jobs that other Americans don't want, taking pressure off employers to pay fair wages. Inflation goes up faster than salaries, and housing costs rise.

None of these factors justify the racism and bigotry that have polluted the American landscape, especially in recent years. But racism and bigotry can spring from a perceived sense of vulnerability, as seen in the "great replacement" conspiracy theory that gets traction in America. This posits a left-wing scheme to replace the White American majority with people of color, including immigrants. Such fear of marginalization creates fertile ground for authoritarian politicians and nativist media outlets to promise that they can fix society by putting snobby professionals, academics, and politicians in their place.

The "great replacement" is an old idea recently taken up by extremist media pundits, White supremacists, and some members of Congress. Demographic patterns indeed are shifting toward greater racial diversity, and I welcome the new landscape. When my neighbor flies a large red flag featuring the name of a presidential candidate I mistrust along with the words "Take Back America," I wince. Take back what from whom?

But that neighbor's spontaneous generosity with the fallen tree established a thread of trust that might be valuable if the time comes to talk about more polarizing matters. I want to extend neighborly kindness to him and to others regardless of their political or social stance. Sometimes the most unlikely persons can change.

A PACIFIST AND A MAJOR GENERAL MEET

I had an unexpected opportunity to see and experience improbable change after an encounter when I was a twenty-five-year-old student at Princeton Theological Seminary. At that time both the United States and the Soviet Union were rapidly expanding their nuclear arsenals and seemed ready to use them. There was widespread fear of nuclear holocaust.

People of the United States became polarized between those who wanted to outmuscle the Soviets and those who wanted to work toward nuclear disarmament. Disparaging anti-nuclear activists, one conservative publication declared there was "not the slightest doubt that this motley crowd is manipulated by a handful of scoundrels instructed directly from Moscow."[6] Leading evangelical preachers promoted "peace through strength," not any plan to freeze production of nuclear weapons.

With this polarized environment, I was unsettled one day to arrive at the seminary chapel and see people on the platform and in the congregation wearing military uniforms. As a Mennonite among Christians of many denominations, I was accustomed to being in a pacifist minority. But this was the seminary's day to honor people in the military, and I felt conflicted about that happening in worship.

The preacher was Maj. Gen. Kermit D. Johnson, West Point graduate, Princeton Theological Seminary graduate, and decorated war veteran. He was chief of chaplains of the US Army, with an office at the Pentagon. He preached from Revelation 22, focusing on the river of the water of life flowing through the New Jerusalem.

Johnson quoted historian Will Durant, who once said the history of the world is a "river red with blood" spilled by political leaders who cause revolutions and wars. "But the real history of the world," Durant said, "takes place on the banks where ordinary people dwell. They are loving one another, bearing children, and providing homes, all the while trying to remain untouched by the swiftly flowing river."[7]

Chaplain Johnson wanted to see a healing of the nations as Revelation describes but said that would require plunging into that river and not just sitting on the bank as pacifists do. I understood that as an argument for Christians to take up arms. After the service I greeted the chaplain, said I was troubled by his sermon, and requested an appointment to talk with him before he left campus. Johnson and his aide arrived at the designated place and time with the seminary president, the seminary dean, and several faculty members. What had I gotten myself into?

The chaplain graciously invited me to set the agenda. Expecting we would have just a few minutes, I wasted no time.

"On one side of your uniform is the cross of Jesus Christ, symbolizing forgiveness and nonviolent love," I began. "On the other side are medals celebrating your proficiency in the arts of killing. How can you hold these two together? Is that not like some early Christians who thought they could give allegiance to Caesar and then follow Jesus?"

Cautious about speaking candidly as a person in his leadership position, the chaplain asked the seminary dean to confirm that I indeed was a student, not a reporter. "So this is off the record?" he asked me. Yes, I said, this would be a confidential conversation between two Christian brothers.

A PENTAGON OFFICIAL STRUGGLES WITH HARD QUESTIONS

Instead of a few minutes, the chaplain gave me an hour. "You have no idea," he began, "how many times, when I walk halls of the Pentagon, these very questions are on my mind." I found that hard to believe, but it was true. The major general who had preached so confidently about "plunging into the river" turned out to have considerable inner struggle about current government policies and his involvement in a military that supported them.

But as the conversation unfolded, the chaplain presented classic "just war" arguments that permit Christians to take up arms for a just cause when authorized by a legitimate government. I countered that little in the New Testament would support that. He agreed but pointed to the fourth century when Emperor Constantine made Christianity the state religion. Once that transformation happened, he declared, Christians had a responsibility to be in government and even in the military to provide moral leadership. "If we don't get involved, persons of less integrity will."

The chaplain and I parted with mutual blessings, then exchanged thank-you letters in a few weeks. A year later, when I was in my first pastorate, a religious news headline caught my eye: "Born-Again Ex-chief Army Chaplain Praises Church Anti-nuclear Stand." It was my chaplain friend; he had left the military. The article said he had converted "from a defender of U.S. nuclear policies to one of their most outspoken critics." Deploring the "idolatry" of nuclear weapons, the former military chaplain declared that Christians "don't have to collaborate with the collective drive toward death."[8]

IF YOU WANT PEACE YOUR CONDUCT MUST SHOW THAT

An interview with Johnson soon appeared in *Sojourners* magazine. It turns out he had been in conversation with many people, and my interaction with him (which he did not mention) must have played only a small part, if any. Johnson had become what people called a nuclear pacifist, not rejecting all use of force but always opposing even the threat of using nuclear weapons. "I became very ill-at-ease at being even a small part of this present U.S. administration," he said (this was during the Reagan presidency). Basic positions of the current government "offend not just my faith but my humanity."[9]

Asked about interaction between military personnel and peace activists, Johnson shared wisdom. "I really bristle when the facile war-mongering stereotype is applied to leaders of the armed forces," he admitted. But both sides in the weapons debate harbored stereotypes, he said. While still in uniform, he became uncomfortable with military personnel who thought of peace activists as "suicidal people who don't really have the best interests of the country at heart and who are unpatriotic, reckless, stupid, not understanding the facts." He found similar stereotypes about military personnel among peace activists.

What did the former military chaplain think about peace movement people and armed forces personnel sitting together for dialogue? It's a good idea, he told *Sojourners*. "But the peace people would have to understand the need for confidentiality and privileged communication. Trust must be present before any dialogue can take place." Building trust is everything when reaching across contested terrain. When I spoke with the chaplain he was still employed by the Pentagon and asked that I not quote him. He died in 2020, and given his public change of heart, I trust he would not object to me telling this story.

Johnson never became a complete pacifist, but I admired his theological and pastoral depth. In the *Sojourners* article, he addressed pacifists: "If you want to speak peace, your life and behavior have to communicate that peace. . . . If we can agree that nuclear idolatry is the most immediate life-threatening danger facing humankind, we can work in partnership to remove this menace."

Several years after his departure from the military, Johnson published theological reflections in a book called *Realism and Hope in a Nuclear Age*. He had recently been interviewed by local television in a politically conservative part of the United States, and the piece aired with a flash across the screen that read, "Chaplain (Major General) Kermit D. Johnson, U.S. Army, Retired—turncoat."[10] In the book he describes himself getting caught in American society's polarization between "warrior" and "peacemaker."

While he was convinced that most military people do not want war, Johnson also came to respect activists who labored for peace and even committed civil disobedience. He lamented that "each side scorns the other side as barely human, which explains why these worlds so rarely come into direct contact with one another. They would rather keep a cold distance, firing rhetorical salvos from long range."[11] Johnson saw the same accusatory distancing happening between the United States and the Soviet Union. He called for visionary politicians and bold prophets to bridge what he saw as a dangerous divide between warriors and peacemakers, and between nuclear superpowers.

ONE ENCOUNTER MADE A LIFELONG IMPRESSION

That encounter with Chaplain Johnson when I was a young adult made a lifelong impression on me. A man I expected to be rigid in politics and theology turned out to have convictions in flux even though he did not reveal that in public. The army chaplain who became a peace activist still comes to mind when I relate to someone whom I experience as politically or theologically rigid. The set face we humans present to the public sometimes masks inner struggle or doubts. We all are in process, taking in new data and dealing with new challenges. It is good for debate to percolate even within our own souls.

It pays to listen closely to someone with whom we disagree, and to convey respect. "Deep listening is an act of surrender," writes civil rights activist and Sikh faith leader Valarie Kaur. "We risk being changed by what we hear." She allows that it is extremely difficult to listen well to someone whose beliefs we find abhorrent or terrifying. But the most critical part of listening is asking *what is at stake* for the other person. As Kaur notes, "The goal of listening is not to feel empathy for our opponents, or validate their ideas, or even change their mind in the moment. Our goal is to understand them." What life experiences or deep needs shape the perspectives of the other person? Kaur emphasizes that listening well "does not grant the other side legitimacy. It grants them humanity—and preserves our own."[12]

I admire Chaplain Johnson for listening carefully to Jesus, for listening to persons on both sides of what was a fraught divide in American society, and for having the courage to change. I want to be just as open to change through relationships God brings into my life. If individuals can be transformed by encountering "the other," can whole churches and societies change?

Chapter 5
REFLECT AND DISCUSS

1. Can you recount a situation when one person's prophetic words or actions represented a threat to the established political or religious order? What happened to the prophet? Did any kind of "track two" diplomacy take place?

2. Have you flown a flag on your vehicle or at your home? If so, what statement did you intend to make? Does it matter which flag—Canadian? American? Confederate? Thin Blue Line? What bumper stickers make you uneasy, and why? How does your gender, race, or economic status shape your response?

3. Relate an incident where someone you assumed would be hostile turned out to be open to conversation. Did unexpected friendship or kindness emerge from that encounter?

4. In what ways do people on the political or theological right and left mirror the others' attitudes or behavior? What stereotyping have you witnessed between polarized groups? How can you tell when stereotyping is happening?

5. What questions does this chapter raise for you?

6

THE BIG CHALLENGE
IS *to* LISTEN WELL

In the early 1990s, when I was director of the London Mennonite Centre in England, I received an anxious phone call from the congregational chair of a Baptist church in Wales. The church was painfully polarized over a vision for congregational direction that the pastor had presented, and someone had said Mennonites do conflict mediation. Could I help? I agreed to make several visits to the church.

My conflict mediation toolbox was minimal, so we focused on the most basic of conflict transformation objectives: getting parties in disagreement to hear each other. Each faction first caucused separately to agree on what frustrated them and what their underlying concerns or desires were. Then the two factions presented these insights to each other. Somebody in each group was designated to summarize what the other side had said until the other side agreed that they had been heard. That simple act of careful listening lowered tension. After several group sessions the pastor agreed to dial back his vision so the entire congregation could decide direction together.

OUR BIGGEST PROBLEM IS FAILING TO LISTEN WELL

In polarized groups or communities, the most common problem is failure to listen well. Having an abundance of options for where we receive information and opinion, we too easily remain in our own ideological or theological comfort zones. Conflict transformation practitioners deploy strategies that help us hear and understand why others choose different zones. Putting these into action requires a desire to bridge the breach of strained relationships. These practices, ideally under the guidance of a trained facilitator, commonly include

1. Listening well to the other party without interrupting their narrative.
2. Making "I/we" statements rather than "you" statements that sound accusatory.
3. Summarizing what the other party has said and seeking their confirmation that they have been heard.
4. Looking for underlying mutual interests and agreeing on ways to address needs of both sides.

Such a process resonates with Matthew 18:15–20, where Jesus sets out four steps for addressing conflict with another individual in the church:

1. Go alone to the person with whom you disagree and state your concern.
2. If that doesn't resolve the matter, try again, taking one or two others with you.
3. If there is still no satisfactory outcome, take the matter to the whole church.
4. If the offender rejects the church's decision, treat that person "as a Gentile and a tax collector" (18:17).

If step 4 sounds harsh, bear in mind that Jesus showed love to Gentiles and tax collectors. Treating persons who ignore counsel from the congregation as Gentiles and tax collectors is not license to hate or despise them. It may be an indication, however, that they effectively give allegiance elsewhere.

HAVE WE MISUNDERSTOOD MATTHEW 18?

The Matthew 18 passage is likely not only about dealing with personal injury or wounded feelings between Christians. Jesus is apparently asking us to approach one another carefully and with direct address if we believe that the other has sinned by making a *wrong moral choice*. Translations of Matthew 18:15 typically say, "If another member of the church sins against you, go and point out the fault when the two of you are alone." But most translations also add a footnote that reads "Other ancient authorities lack *against you*." The earliest ancient manuscripts simply say, "If another member of the church *sins*, go and point out the fault . . ."

I am persuaded by the shorter version: Jesus is calling us to speak to a Christian sister or brother *who we believe has sinned*. When ancient New Testament authorities (manuscripts of the Bible) disagree on the wording of a particular verse, scholars tend to prefer the shorter version. This is on the assumption that scribes making the ancient copies were more likely to have added to the sacred text than to have subtracted from it. Scribes copying Matthew 18:15 may have tried to be helpful by adding *against you*, but that significantly limits the meaning of the text.

Reference to sin often accompanies conflicts in the church today, especially in relation to sexual and gender minorities. The focus on sexual minorities contrasts with Jesus, who had more concern about greed, truth-telling, enemies, judgmentalism, and hypocrisy—matters that do not get as much attention in most churches today.

Regardless of our political or theological views, Jesus in Matthew 18 authorizes us to speak to fellow church members who we believe have made wrong moral choices, but to do so in love. This is person-to-person mutual accountability within the congregation. Church leaders may get involved eventually, but that generally is not where the response of the faith community should start.

Jesus taught, "Why do you see the speck in your neighbor's eye, but do not notice the log in your own eye?" (Matthew 7:3). This teaching stands out like a blinking amber light reminding us to be cautious. It is best to think things through carefully before calling fellow Christians to account, and to not rush to confront. Listening well is our primary goal, not delivering judgment.

Considering such direct address in situations of sin comes with a caveat: It is not wise for someone who has been physically, emotionally, or sexually abused to go directly to the perpetrator. Such situations usually involve differences of power that make survivors of abuse likely to be further harmed by attempting direct address. It is appropriate for persons who have been targeted to speak to a trusted confidant such as a pastor, teacher, or professional counselor. An abuser is likely to manipulate.

CONGREGATIONS HAVE AUTHORITY TO DO MORAL DISCERNMENT

If confidential conversation with a person we believe has sinned does not resolve the concern, the disagreement appropriately becomes a matter for communal discernment. Jesus gives congregations extraordinary authority to decide about moral issues. "Whatever you bind on earth will be bound in heaven," he declared, "and whatever you loose on earth will be loosed in heaven." Because Christians have so often applied Matthew 18:15–20 to situations of personal injury, we miss the congregational policy-making aspect of Jesus' teaching. The Greek word translated as "bind" is a legal term meaning compel, restrict, or prohibit; the Greek word rendered as "loose" means to set free, dismiss, or permit.

The most literal translation of the Greek text in this passage would be "Whatever you prohibit on earth *will have been prohibited* in heaven, and whatever you permit on earth *will have been permitted* in heaven."[1] Does this mean that heaven ratifies what the church decides, guided by the Spirit? Or does it mean that the church only has latitude to decide what heaven permits? In either case, Jesus gives the church authority for moral discernment and boundary-setting. The Lord who taught us to pray "Your will be done on earth as it is in heaven" now seems to say that heaven ratifies what the church decides.

This cannot mean that mere congregational consensus validates *anything*; whole congregations or denominations can err by cutting loose from confessional or biblical moorings. The apostle Paul insists, for example, that "no one speaking by the Spirit of God ever says, 'Let Jesus be cursed!'" (1 Corinthians 12:3). There are confessional, ethical, or justice boundaries that congregations cannot cross while remaining faithful. But Jesus' teaching about church authority to bind and loose makes it inevitable that God's people will come down at different places in belief and practice.

In recent decades, discernment about the role of LGBTQ people in the church has generated debate and division. I am deeply troubled by the suffering that LGBTQ individuals have endured as the body of Christ has had prolonged and

rancorous debate about their basic identity. But I am not surprised that congregations and whole denominations vary in
what they understand sexual orientation and gender identity
to mean. Division over boundaries has been part of the church
from the beginning.

THERE ARE MANY GIFTS AND MANY PERSPECTIVES IN ONE FAITH COMMUNITY

Was any congregation in the early church more fractured than
the church at Corinth? The city was an international trade hub
percolating with upwardly mobile people from diverse cultures. This flavored the church. Division, idolatry, and sexual
immorality roiled the group, and Paul wrote multiple letters
trying to rein in the chaos.

Paul tells the rambunctious Corinthians that "there are
varieties of gifts, but the same Spirit" (1 Corinthians 12:4).
We usually interpret this as meaning a variety of *abilities* such
as teaching, administration, or financial management. But
what if we saw this human body metaphor as also represent-
ing diverse theological and biblical *perspectives*? Paul hints at
such a meaning:

> To each is given the manifestation of the Spirit for the com-
> mon good. To one is given through the Spirit the utterance
> of wisdom, and to another the utterance of knowledge ac-
> cording to the same Spirit, . . . to another prophecy, to an-
> other the discernment of spirits. . . . All these are activated
> by one and the same Spirit, who allots to each one individ-
> ually just as the Spirit chooses. (1 Corinthians 12:7–11)

These are not only multiple offices, but multiple *perspectives*. The Spirit imparts wisdom to one person and knowledge to another. Prophets speak and others interpret. Chaotic

as this sounds, if the Spirit is at work, it is for the common good. Elsewhere, Paul tells Corinthian believers that "the Lord [Jesus] is the Spirit, and where the Spirit of the Lord is, there is freedom" (2 Corinthians 3:17).

Using such freedom requires faith communities to exercise discernment, a skill that pastor and theologian Richard Kauffman believes the church needs to recover. "Too many Christians have made a fateful turn from dealing with conflictual issues through discernment to using advocacy instead," he asserts. "Discernment is collaborative, while acknowledging difference and disagreement. Advocacy assumes that *my position is correct, and the rest need to come over to me.*"[2] Advocacy may be helpful, but in the end, the faith community functions best by corporate discernment.

THE CHURCH NEEDS PROPHETS EVEN IF THEY ARE DISRUPTIVE

The apostle Paul's mention of prophets brings to mind people in the church who carry placards at denominational assemblies to protest the exclusion of minorities, and advocates who demand that the church address institutional racism and environmental degradation. Having been an administrator for several church institutions, I can testify that prophets sometimes feel disruptive. Like the Sadducees who ran the temple, church administrators struggle to balance diverse constituencies, traditions, and fiscal realities. Stability seems like a good thing.

But the church needs prophets as much as it needs administrators. When Paul enumerates various players in the life of the church, prophets rank high. He says God has appointed "first apostles, second prophets, third teachers." The list goes on, and administrators rank *seventh* as persons with "forms of leadership" (1 Corinthians 12:28). Institutional leaders such as monarchs and priests in the Old Testament were often in tension with prophets, who were likely to speak from the margins of the faith community. Elijah found himself on the king and queen's hit list; Jeremiah got thrown into a dungeon.

God's people need both administrators and prophets—and a lot of other participants. With this mix of roles and perspectives, it is holy work for the church to discern God's will on issues of faith and morality. Discernment calls for prayer, openness to the Spirit, counsel of a community, guidance from scripture, insight of previous generations, and patience. Sometimes it is wise to take "time out" from prolonged discernment. But it is precisely when we are in the midst of conflict that Jesus assures us, "Where two or three are gathered in my name, I am there among them" (Matthew 18:20).

OUR HOPE IS IN KNOWING THE POWER OF CHRIST'S RESURRECTION

In his letter to the Philippians, the apostle Paul is scathing toward fellow believers who insist that the church require Gentile Christians to observe the whole of Jewish law. Angry at those who demand that Gentiles be circumcised, Paul says, "Beware of the dogs . . . who mutilate the flesh!" (Philippians 3:2). Elsewhere he adds, "I wish those who unsettle you would castrate themselves!" (Galatians 5:12).

Whew! Those are bitter words, suggesting that the apostle struggled as much as any of us with anger in the maelstrom of polarization. But then, after rehearsing his spiritual pedigree in Philippians 3 only to dismiss it as irrelevant, Paul goes to the heart of the gospel: "I want to know Christ and the power of his resurrection and the sharing of his sufferings by becoming like him in his death" (3:10). This, Paul says, is the path to hope. Knowing Christ is the prize which Paul most deeply desires.

With his relentless energy and keen intellect, the apostle must have been intimidating sometimes. "We destroy arguments and every proud obstacle raised up against the knowledge of God," he told the Corinthians (2 Corinthians 10:4–5). No wonder opponents were ready to take him down a notch, sneering, "His letters are weighty and strong, but his bodily presence is weak, and his speech contemptible" (10:10). The second-century *Acts of Paul and Thecla* says, "He was a man of middling size, and his hair was scanty, and his legs were a little crooked, and his knees were projecting; and he had large eyes and his eyebrows met, and his nose was somewhat long." Yet "he was full of grace and mercy."[3]

Paul rarely missed an opportunity to assert himself on contested issues, but occasionally seems to remind himself that others also have insight. After giving Christians at Philippi counsel on various matters, he says, "If you think differently about anything, this too God will reveal to you. Only let us hold fast to what we have attained" (Philippians 3:15–16). I take "what we have attained" to be points of agreement that the apostle had even with some opponents. Beyond those points of convergence, Paul seems to acknowledge that God may reveal something different to others. He tells the Philippians to "work out your own salvation with fear and trembling; for it is God who is at work in you" (Philippians 2:12–13).

SOMETIMES A FAITH COMMUNITY NEEDS TO DECIDE

Diversity alone is not an adequate identity for the church. When disputed theological or ethical matters challenge or compromise foundations of the faith community, God's people especially need to discern and make choices. Are changes of understanding about sexuality evidence of God's Spirit at work or signs of moral decay? How should Christians respond to the rising tide of political personality cult in America? When does healthy patriotism become idolatry? Do ancient doctrines of the atonement or the Trinity still matter? What should be our response to the growing chasm between rich and poor? The author of 1 John instructs believers to "test the spirits to see whether they are from God" (1 John 4:1). The church at Corinth learned they should "let two or three prophets speak, and let the others weigh what is said" (1 Corinthians 14:29–30). That requires corporate discernment.

From the Presbyterian tradition comes a handbook for such holy work: *Guidelines for Communal Discernment* by Victoria G. Curtiss.[4] The author recommends discernment rather than debate. In debate, she says, participants want to resolve issues "by defeating or persuading the opposing side." But through good discernment, groups discover "what is most life-giving and loving by listening to wisdom of the Holy Spirit and all voices."[5] Such discernment requires disciplined work by leaders and participants:

> Prayer is incorporated throughout, with times of silence for listening to the Holy Spirit. The interpretation and application of Scripture is central. Time is taken to hear many voices. Values, concerns, hopes, and fears are named more than positions. Intuition, experience, reason, tradition, and new insights are all welcome sources for reflection. Common direction is sought through cooperation and collaboration. Discernment seeks more than group agreement. The goal is to recognize when "it has seemed good to the Holy Spirit and to us." (Acts 15:28)[6]

Curtiss gives step-by-step counsel on how such discernment can happen. Appendixes at the back of her book include community trust-building tools, prayer and hymn resources, ways to engage scripture, and more.

LIVE INTO THE HOPE THAT GOD WILL RECONCILE ALL THINGS

In his recent book *The Church of Us vs. Them*, evangelical theologian David Fitch laments the current "strife, antagonisms, and vitriol" in North American society. But he grieves even more that Christians "appear to be caught up in the same antagonism and disgust for one another that is evident elsewhere." Addressing that disfunction within the church is essential for proclaiming the gospel in society, Fitch contends. To be effective, "we must first become the place the world can recognize as beyond enemies. We must first deal with our own antagonisms. Once freed, we then can enter the world in peace, opening up space for Christ to work."[7]

Inspired by the vision that God is reconciling to himself all things (Colossians 1:20), in 2011 a group of Christians concerned about polarization in the church founded the Colossian Forum and its Colossian Way process. Their goal is to "gather Christians together, practice loving God and neighbor while engaging difficult problems, and witness the body of Christ built up."[8] In practical terms, that means training pastors and lay leaders to guide Christian groups through ten ninety-minute sessions that address an issue the group finds difficult.

The Colossian Way has helped congregations address differences over sexuality, origins of the cosmos, politics, and more. Board member Kristi Potter says their mission "is to help Christians act like Christ in times of conflict."[9] Michael Gulker, president, draws inspiration from theology of the incarnation. "We cannot love each other in the abstract," he insists, "we need the embodied life. Difficult conversation can be an act of worship where, instead of trying to win, the goal is deeper love of God, deeper love of neighbor, and fruit of the Spirit."[10]

The Colossian Forum provides outstanding resources and theological depth. But addressing theological conflicts by such a group process encounters a problem familiar to politics: the progressive/liberal sector usually wants to orchestrate the conversation and keep it going until there is desired change of some kind. Conservatives, who tend to want to conserve, are disposed to resist change, and get impatient with endless processing.

That dynamic makes it important for persons who hold liberal values and those who hold conservative values to work together in planning, promoting, and facilitating conversation. With good training and spiritual sensitivity, leaders can create safe space for persons with contrasting perspectives to hear and respect each other.

BRAVER ANGELS FLY INTO RED AND BLUE TURMOIL

While the Colossian Way fosters good communication among Christians, something similar also can happen in secular settings. When the United States became bitterly divided in the wake of the 2016 presidential election, political alienation fractured families, churches, and communities. Democrat and Republican neighbors were not talking to each other. That concerned several men in Ohio who, though coming from opposite ends of the political spectrum, thought that alienation in society was a problem. Using techniques developed by marriage therapists, they assembled ten Donald Trump supporters and eleven Hillary Clinton supporters for conversation. The idea of this first "Red/Blue Workshop" was simply to see whether participants could disagree respectfully.

Out of that experiment grew a national organization called Braver Angels. A summer bus tour launched the idea, a regular podcast followed, and now Braver Angels has chapters in all fifty states. Trained volunteers guide group conversations with people who otherwise might ignore, despise, or even hate each other. The Braver Angels Pledge captures the spirit of this project:

- As individuals, we try to understand the other side's point of view, even if we don't agree with it.
- In our communities, we engage those we disagree with, looking for common ground and ways to work together.
- In politics, we support principles that bring us together rather than divide us.[11]

Braver Angels president David Blankenhorn contrasts dialogue and debate. People in debates "are not expected to change their views as result of the debate. Quite the opposite: They are expected to try to change *other* people's views." But in dialogue, "you no longer take your own position as final. You relax your grip on certainty and listen to the possibilities that result simply from being in a relationship with others." Dialogue, unlike debate, "usually incorporates the participants' personal experiences and feelings as well as their abstractly formulated philosophical positions."[12]

Liberals tend to promote dialogue, Blankenhorn says, and conservatives often prefer debate. He observes that the "entire concept and practice of dialogue—who funds it, who studies and writes about it, who advocates for it, who designs it, who convenes it, and who leads it—is overwhelmingly blue [liberal]." Add to this the reluctance of many conservatives to participate in a process where it is expected or hoped that they will change their views.

Because the word *dialogue* has become so "deeply blue," Blankenhorn prefers not to use it when fostering interaction across the political divide. He suggests *workshop* instead, asking why it would be helpful to signal in advance that participants are likely to "change and grow" from the exchange. If change is going to happen, why not simply allow it to take place organically?[13] Braver Angels is a forum where Christians can and should participate as part of our witness to the world.

Chapter 6
REFLECT AND DISCUSS

1. Has the church changed its processes for discernment on disputed moral or ethical matters during your lifetime? If so, how?

2. Can you give an example of when you were heard well by others during a dispute? When you were not heard well? How did good or poor listening by others affect your feelings or the outcome of the dispute?

3. When have you seen prophets work effectively and wisely in the church? How did their ministry intersect with corporate discernment by the faith community? Have you ever been a prophet?

4. Why or why not would you participate in a Colossian Way or Braver Angels process?

5. What questions does this chapter raise for you?

OUR STORIES CHANGE HOW WE READ *the* BIBLE

Regardless of whether you think church and society are changing views on sexuality too slowly or too quickly, you probably will agree that the change has been polarizing. Marriage for gay couples, transgender people in sports, leadership by LGBTQ people, and other matters related to sexuality and gender identity or expression generate contentious debate in secular and religious settings. Wounds are deep for individuals in church and society whose experience of sexuality or gender differs from the majority. A 2020 survey showed that within the previous year, 40 percent of LGBTQ youth had contemplated suicide.[1] That should awaken the church to the pain we can either make worse or help alleviate.

PARENTS OF A GAY MAN EXPERIENCE A CHANGING CHURCH

Esther and Jim, long committed to the mission of the church, agreed to share in a formal interview how they have experienced sexuality debates in their denomination.[2] Both grew up in conservative communities where people viewed the Bible as authoritative and did not accept same-sex intimacy. When the movement to admit such unions gained strength in church and society, Jim was concerned. "I grew up with a 'bounded' church," he said. "Boundaries were appropriate and necessary. Separation from values of the world was good. Was the idea of blessing same-sex relationships just the faith community conforming to changing values of society?"

Jim was alarmed when his denomination began to divide. "When I saw LGBTQ advocates lobbying at our denominational assembly, I was not pleased," he recalled. "A struggling denomination did not need that issue at such a critical moment." Esther added that she never had strong convictions about gay and lesbian people in the church. "I simply did not think about it much," she said. "I was a quiet bystander."

Knowing that Esther and Jim are now ready to see the church bless same-sex unions, I asked what had changed. "We attended our denominational assembly," Esther said, "and came upon an impromptu hymn sing in the hallway. The music was led by people wearing pink shirts that identified them as LGBTQ advocates. The group was singing beloved hymns in heartfelt and joyous worship."

Jim and Esther's young adult child had recently come out as gay. There was no question that they would continue to love their child, and this factored large in their thinking. But the hymn sing was a transforming moment, and Jim's eyes welled as he remembered. "Here were gay and lesbian people who, against all odds, wanted to be part of a church that didn't want them. They were worshiping outside the gates, so to speak, leading God's people in worship. I got a glimpse of that great chorus in heaven of people from every tribe and nation." Jim's denomination was excluding part of the chorus, and he could not give "one more crank of the wheel of division" by rejecting them.

POLARIZATION OVER SEXUALITY AFFECTS MANY FAITH COMMUNITIES

Differences in understandings about sexuality have brought division among many church bodies. A sadly familiar pattern emerges: denominations that long have recognized only covenanted heterosexual marriage face internal challenge from LGBTQ advocates who view traditional sexual boundaries as un-Christlike. Some congregations, disregarding standards of their denomination, decide to bless covenanted same-sex unions. There are calls for denominational discipline or for a change in church regulations.

Discernment processes follow. Conservatives promote what they see as biblical principles supporting traditional marriage while progressives call for what they see as biblical principles of grace and freedom in Christ. One side gains control of institutions in a diminished denomination, and those in disagreement exit to form or join what they view as a more faithful communion.

Some denominations have coped with this polarization by developing affinity-defined conferences ("middle judicatories") in addition to geographically defined structures. Members of affinity-defined conferences network with each other across the continent rather than relate to nearby members of their own denomination who hold different views. Perhaps having such "flying bishops" is the best we can do, but that mirrors the world's weary pattern of people sorting themselves into ideological echo chambers. Such divisions are akin to divorce, and may separate us from contrasting perspectives we may need.

Just hours before he died, Jesus prayed that his followers would "become completely one, so that the world may know that you [the Father] have sent me and have loved them even

as you have loved me" (John 17:23). Jesus' desire that his followers *become* one suggests that he knew we would struggle
with division. He did not pray that we would always agree,
but that we stay together in the same love that bound Jesus
to the Father. We stay together "so that the world may know."

I was moved by Esther and Jim's story of how their view
of same-sex relationships shifted when they experienced
Christ-centered worship among advocates for gay and lesbian
inclusion. But should the church decide ethical and moral matters strictly on the basis of emotional experiences? What about
Bible passages that seem to reject homosexual practice?

The Bible doesn't say much about homosexuality, and
speaks only tangentially about the matter when it does. That
is, homosexuality is not the main topic of any Bible passage,
but when it is mentioned it is usually an illustration or result
of something else—such as humanity worshiping and serving
"the creature rather than the Creator" (see Romans 1:24–27).
There is no evidence that Bible writers even thought of the
possibility of covenanted same-sex unions. In the Greek and
Roman cultures of the New Testament era, homosexuality
usually meant a man with social or economic power exploiting an enslaved or freeborn boy.[3]

JEWISH VIEWS OF SEXUALITY INFLUENCED EARLY CHRISTIANITY

The Jewish culture from which Christian faith emerged
rejected homosexual practice. Philo of Alexandria, prolific
Jewish author in the first century, condemned same-sex intimacy.[4] In his understanding, such relationships happened primarily at drunken orgies either with male prostitutes or with
boys made to look like women. He and other Jewish teachers
thought homosexuality made men effeminate and, since it did

not produce offspring, undermined the biblical mandate to be fruitful and multiply. Citing Leviticus 20:13, Philo declared that homosexual violators of the Law of Moses should be put to death.

The apostle Paul, who wrote all of what little appears in the New Testament on same-sex intimacy, reflects typical Jewish understandings of his time. It is not clear what kind of same-sex relationships Paul had in mind with his negative comments (Romans 1:26–32; 1 Corinthians 6:9–11), because he only incidentally alludes to the topic. We have no record of Jesus saying anything about homosexuality.

WE APPLY UNEVEN STANDARDS WHEN WE READ THE BIBLE

Jim and Esther reflected on the few Bible verses commonly understood as rejecting homosexual practice. "I recently read Exodus," Jim said, "and got to thinking about how we apply that book. The church is familiar with the commandment to keep the Sabbath holy, but we read only one version of that mandate. A second version says, 'Whoever does any work on the sabbath day shall be put to death' [Exodus 31:15]. Put to death! If we obeyed that, there would be a lot of dead Christians."

All Christians make choices about which parts of scripture we give particular weight and which passages we use to interpret others. I join many other Christians in believing that the church should read the whole Bible through the prism of Jesus' teaching and example. In the eyes of devout first-century Jews, Jesus broke Mosaic laws regarding persons with leprosy, the Sabbath, and contact with "sinners." As Matthew 12:1–8 recounts, when his disciples were hungry while passing through a grainfield on the Sabbath, Jesus did not stop them from helping themselves to handfuls of grain. That "work" violated rabbinic interpretation of the biblical mandate not to labor on the Sabbath, and Pharisees complained.

Jesus responded by reminding listeners that David once ate sacred "bread of the Presence" from the tabernacle when he and his fellow bandits were hungry (1 Samuel 21:1–6). Human need required David to make flexible application of biblical law. Similarly, Jesus implied, his hungry disciples appropriately harvested a small amount of grain on the Sabbath. Quoting Hosea, Jesus declared that God desires "mercy and not sacrifice" (Hosea 6:6 NKJV).

THE INTENT OF THE LAW IS RIGHTEOUSNESS AND JUSTICE

"Do not think that I have come to abolish the Law or the Prophets," Jesus said. "I have come not to abolish but to fulfill" (Matthew 5:17). Jesus fulfilled the Law and the Prophets, not by repudiating them, or by enforcing them with wooden literalism, but by empowering believers to live into the righteousness/justice *intent* of scripture. Even though the apostle Paul declares that "Christ is the end of the law" (Romans 10:4), the Greek word (*telos*) that he uses for "end" can mean either termination or culmination/goal. The latter meaning aligns Paul with Jesus in fulfilling the purpose of the law.

"For freedom Christ has set us free," the apostle Paul declares. "Stand firm, therefore, and do not submit again to a yoke of slavery" (Galatians 5:1). Here Paul refers to the bondage of a legalistic view of scripture and tradition that required even Gentiles coming into the church to accept circumcision and full adherence to the Law of Moses. The apostle's treatment of issues facing the church reflects his deep knowledge of scripture, which is "God-breathed" and "useful for teaching, rebuking, correcting and training in righteousness (2 Timothy 3:16 NIV)." Today's church needs a similar focus on scripture—not as proof-texts to bludgeon others, but as the most useful window into God's will.

THE EARLY CHURCH SETTLES A POLARIZING ISSUE

In the New Testament there is one narrative (Acts 10–15) that shows step-by-step how the early church worked through a divisive issue.[5] This was a fierce disagreement over the extent to which Gentiles had to conform to Jewish law when joining the church. It is hard for us today to comprehend how big a hurdle this was for the first generation of believers, all of whom were Jews following a Jewish messiah who they believed fulfilled the Jewish scriptures.

With considerable effort, Gentiles could become Jewish, but they had to accept circumcision and the whole of the Law of Moses. At the end of his public ministry, Paul nearly got lynched when devout Jews in Jerusalem accused him of bringing uncircumcised Gentiles into exclusive precincts of the temple (Acts 21:27–36). But bringing Gentiles into the temple at Jerusalem was not Paul's goal. Rather, he wanted Gentiles and all who confessed Jesus as Lord accepted *into the church*. He wanted the church to receive them as fellow heirs to God's promises regardless of the extent to which they observed ritual aspects of Jewish law.

Even fellow Christians initially opposed this open stance, because it seemed to directly violate the teachings of the Hebrew Scriptures. In traditional understanding, God had made circumcision the central marker of fidelity to the "everlasting covenant" with Abraham and his descendants. Any male who rejected the rite, God declared, had "broken my covenant" (Genesis 17:9–14).

Clear as Old Testament teaching seemed to be, the experience of the early church began to rattle long-held Jewish beliefs. What was the apostle Peter to make of the Holy Spirit being poured out upon an uncircumcised Roman centurion at an army base in Caesarea (Acts 10)? When Cornelius and other Gentiles at Caesarea confessed Jesus as Lord and began praising the God of Israel in tongues, Peter promptly baptized them. He acted when the power and presence of God became evident.

NARRATIVE HAS AN IMPORTANT ROLE IN CHURCH DECISION-MAKING

Narratives of such encounters with Gentiles played an important part in early Christian leaders consenting for uncircumcised people to be part of the church. When Peter encountered criticism at Jerusalem from followers of Jesus who demanded strict adherence to the Law of Moses, Peter told what happened at Joppa and Caesarea. Hearing the story of the centurion Cornelius tipped the debate, and at least some Jewish believers at Jerusalem saw for the first time that "God has given even the Gentiles the repentance that leads to life" (Acts 11:18). Similarly, when Paul and Barnabas returned to Antioch after their mission to Asia and Galatia, they "called the church together and related all that God had done with them, and how he had opened a door of faith for the Gentiles" (Acts 14:27).

Neither Peter nor Paul intended to operate as independent agents; they wanted accountability to the sending churches at Antioch and Jerusalem. Formal accountability happened after "certain individuals" came down to Antioch from Jerusalem to oppose the idea that uncircumcised Gentiles could be saved. Seeking wider counsel, believers at Antioch sent Paul,

Barnabas, and others to Jerusalem to consult with church leaders there (Acts 15).

Storytelling continued as the delegation traveled through Phoenicia and Samaria, where they "reported the conversion of the Gentiles, and brought great joy to all the believers" (15:3). Again, when Paul and company got to the church at Jerusalem, they "reported all that God had done with them" (15:4). Certain Pharisees who believed in Jesus, however, still opposed an open stance toward Gentiles.

Senior leaders of the Jerusalem church convened a meeting to discern a way forward. There was "much debate" (15:7), after which Peter took the floor and began more storytelling: God had called him to share the gospel beyond the boundaries of Judaism, and God had validated uncircumcised Gentile believers by giving them the Holy Spirit. Why, Peter asked, would the church then insist that they bear a "yoke" that God did not require? The gathered leaders remained silent while Barnabas and Paul "told of all the signs and wonders that God had done through them among the Gentiles" (15:12).

Experience-followed-by-storytelling-followed-by-new-insight-on-scripture is a sequence that happens repeatedly in the New Testament and in the church today. Devout Jewish people met the risen Christ, told fellow Jews about their encounters, and then figured out from scripture what God was doing in Jesus of Nazareth. Saul on his way to Damascus encountered the risen Christ, told the story to the Christian community, and only later understood that this was fulfillment of scripture.[6] Early missionaries saw Gentiles receiving the Holy Spirit, told the story to fellow Christians, and then read scriptures in a new way. Esther and Jim experienced God's presence in their child and among LGBTQ advocates and then read scripture differently.

DISCERNMENT NEEDS TO BE GROUNDED IN THE WITNESS OF SCRIPTURE

Early Jewish followers of Jesus knew the Hebrew Scriptures well; they were not operating in a vacuum devoid of biblical knowledge. Scrolls were cumbersome and expensive, so we often see early Christian leaders simply quoting scripture from memory. After listening to narratives that Peter and Paul presented at Jerusalem, for example, James alluded to relevant texts from Jeremiah, Amos, and Isaiah.

Events reported from the mission field had opened James's eyes to see what it meant for God to "rebuild the dwelling of David . . . so that all other peoples may seek the Lord—even all the Gentiles" (Acts 15:16–17; cf. Amos 9:11–12).[7] These few quotes from the Old Testament seem like slim basis for a major shift in faith community boundaries, but they likely were only a sample of the biblical background that informed early church decisions.

With narratives of God's surprising activity bringing new insight to scripture, James proposed a way forward: The church would not demand that Gentile believers accept circumcision, but would still expect them to observe other central aspects of the Law of Moses—to avoid idols, sexual immorality,[8] "strangled" meat (meat not prepared in the kosher manner), and "blood" (likely a dietary restriction).

This proposal was a compromise, and it carried the day. Innovators who wanted to receive uncircumcised Gentiles into the church could do so, but Gentiles needed to respect Jewish sensibilities regarding monotheism, sexual morality, and kosher food. The food requirement was important if Jewish and Gentile believers were to continue sharing eucharist meals.

Having reached consensus, the Jerusalem assembly sent a letter to churches in Antioch, Syria, and Cilicia declaring that it "seemed good to the Holy Spirit and to us" not to demand circumcision of Gentile believers, but rather to require adherence only to several specific prohibitions.

A SUMMARY OF THE DISCERNMENT PROCESS AT THE ACTS 15 MEETING

Here in sum are steps early Christian leaders took to decide a divisive question:[9]

1. Leaders recognized growing tension within the church. "Certain individuals" differed with Paul and Barnabas on the question of circumcision, and "no small dissension and debate" arose (Acts 15:1–2).

2. The church created a forum to hear all parties in the dispute. The faith community in Antioch appointed "Paul and Barnabas and some of the others . . . to go up to Jerusalem to discuss this question with the apostles and the elders" (15:2).

3. People involved in the conflict had opportunity to tell their stories. The delegation arrived at Jerusalem and "reported all that God had done with them" (15:4).

4. There was adequate time to air convictions and perspectives. There was "much debate" (15:7).

5. Someone proposed a way forward that aligned with scripture and addressed concerns raised by both sides. "After they finished speaking, James replied, 'My brothers . . . I have reached the decision that we should not trouble [with circumcision] those Gentiles who are turning to God, but we should write to them to abstain only from things polluted by idols and from fornication and from whatever has been strangled'" (15:13, 19–21).

6. Participants in the forum ratified the proposed solution by consensus. With the "consent of the whole church," the leaders at Jerusalem sent a delegation to scattered congregations to convey agreements reached (see 15:22–25).

The fact that the final decision "seemed good to the Holy Spirit and to us" (15:28) implies that discernment included prayer or some other mode of spiritual attentiveness.

THERE MAY BE A BREADTH OF SPIRIT-INSPIRED PERSPECTIVES TODAY

Blessing same-sex relationships in the church today is not a direct parallel to inclusion of uncircumcised Gentiles in the early church. We cannot argue that the Acts 10–15 model means the church must become "affirming." Some churches will use an Acts 10–15 process and come to liberal conclusions while others take the same steps and come to conservative conclusions. If the Holy Spirit can inspire a breadth of perspectives within the Bible, it's not surprising that the same would happen in the church today. We are wise not to condemn other Christians who undertake careful discernment processes and end up with contrasting pastoral conclusions.

The Acts 10–15 decision-making model shows the importance of hearing diverse perspectives. Giving voice to all stakeholders must include testimony of how God has worked in the lives of people most affected by the issue at hand. When God's people do discernment with love and patience, conflict can be good. In the words of one New Testament scholar, "Conflict is simply one of the faces of discernment in a community context."[10]

Today, Christians have a resource that early followers of Jesus did not: two thousand years of church experience from previous eras. Such tradition provides ballast to help keep the ship on an even keel. We see the stabilizing role of tradition already within the New Testament, as when Paul tells believers at Corinth, "I commend you because you remember me in everything and maintain the traditions just as I handed them on to you" (1 Corinthians 11:2). When Paul became a believer, he received teaching that he then relayed to Corinth.

Let us never be so parochial as to imagine that our moment in history is so self-contained and complete that we don't need the spiritual riches of previous generations. Tradition, scripture, and experience make the three-legged stool of discernment. To these three John Wesley added reason, creating the so-called Wesleyan Quadrilateral.

Milking stools usually have three legs because four-legged models do not sit well on uneven ground. But the church will face new challenges in every generation, and we need the fourth leg of reason. "Do not despise the words of prophets," Paul told believers at Thessalonica, "but test everything; hold fast to what is good" (1 Thessalonians 5:20–21). Such testing demands reason.

Tradition does not carry the same weight that scripture carries in our discernment. Tradition can be wrong, and every generation can ask whether a particular established precedent is or ever was right. Over the centuries, Christians have shifted understanding of slavery, monarchy, divorce, leadership by women, and more. It is wrong to rush such decision-making, and wrong for any one of us to think that outcomes must conform in every way to what we individually believe.

GOD'S SPIRIT WILL CONTINUE TO CALL US TOGETHER

We should not expect conflict to cease immediately after a faith community decides an issue. A paragraph in Paul's letters shows that he and Peter had an angry exchange at Antioch (Galatians 2:11–14), apparently after the church had decided how to receive Gentiles in Acts 15. The exchange happened when Peter came to Antioch and Paul "opposed him to his face, because he stood self-condemned." Peter had been eating at table with Gentiles, but when conservatives from Jerusalem arrived, he "drew back and kept himself separate for fear of the circumcision faction."

If we let go of the idea that God's people must always agree, we can rest in the confidence that God's Spirit will continue to guide. Jesus told his disciples that the Spirit "will teach you everything and remind you of all that I have said to you" (John 14:26). The Spirit "will guide you [plural] into all truth . . . and will declare to you [plural] the things that are to come" (16:13).

You and I do not create unity in the church; it is a gift that God gives through Christ. "For he is our peace; in his flesh he has made both groups into one and has broken down the dividing wall, that is, the hostility between us" (Ephesians 2:14).

Chapter 7
REFLECT AND DISCUSS

1. Recall a time when you or someone you know faced circumstances that raised ethical or moral questions (an unplanned pregnancy, divorce, coming out as gay or transgender, bankruptcy, being taken to court . . .). In what way did that situation change your perspectives or convictions?

2. How do you weigh verses of the Bible that have been used to reject homosexuality? What about verses with mandates that Christians today reject, such as executing people who work on the Sabbath?

3. For making moral or ethical choices, what part or parts of the Bible particularly speak to you? Why?

4. If you had been a first-century Jew who took the Bible seriously, would you have accepted Paul's argument that Gentiles could come into the faith community without circumcision? If so, what would have been the deciding factor in changing your perspective?

5. What questions does this chapter raise for you?

PAUL BOLDLY BRIDGED *the* JEW-GENTILE POLARITY

During language study in Guatemala in 2009, I made a pilgrimage to the Maya village of Santiago Atitlán in the central highlands. Nestled between scenic volcanoes, this small town was an epicenter of conflict during civil war in the 1980s. Guatemala was a pawn on a global chessboard where empires—especially the United States—strategized for access to resources and political hegemony.

I visited an old Catholic church in Santiago Atitlán, where a large photograph of a priest named Stanley Rother hung at the front of the sanctuary. Below was a quote from this Oklahoma native who spent thirteen years ministering there: "El pastor no debe huir" (The shepherd must not flee).[1] Rother worked with the Tz'utujil people, many of them the poorest of the poor, who resented international corporations taking their land for export crops. Such corporations had backing from the Guatemalan government and, by extension, from the United States.

When twenty members of Rother's congregation disappeared, presumably murdered by death squads, he started a fund to support their families. Showing solidarity with

Indigenous people was risky, and anyone working to eliminate poverty or illiteracy was in danger. "Shaking hands with an Indian has become a political act," Father Rother complained.[2]

Warned that he was on a death list, Rother briefly went back to Oklahoma, but returned to Guatemala just before Holy Week, 1981. "The shepherd must not flee," he told a friend. In July of that year, masked gunmen entered the rectory of his church at Santiago Atitlán at night and shot Father Rother dead. By dawn, a thousand Tz'utujil people gathered in tense silence in front of the church. Sensing that the situation was volatile, a Carmelite sister calmed the restive multitude by leading them in singing resurrection hymns.

THE COURAGE OF PAUL CAN INSPIRE US
TO BE PEACEMAKERS

Are Christians in North America willing to take even small steps to reach across widening chasms in church and society? The courage of martyrs such as Father Rother and the apostle Paul might inspire us to take risks for reconciliation.

Not all of Paul's peacemaking work was life-threatening. He regularly dealt with congregational disputes about matters such as speaking in tongues or eating meat offered to idols. Such disagreements could be heated but didn't approach the explosive power of a larger phenomenon that alarmed devout Jews: the growing number of people who believed that Jesus had opened a way for Gentiles to become heirs to the promises of Israel without full compliance to Torah law. No one in the early church was a greater proponent of this development than Paul, and that put him in danger. Changing the boundaries of Judaism made him suspect to fellow Jews and to Roman authorities.[3]

At stake were fundamental questions of Jewish identity and ethnic survival: What did it mean to be Jewish after centuries of living under foreign control? Was God punishing Israel again by allowing a series of empires to trample it, and were God's people now forsaken? Divine favor now seemed to be on Rome's side. Josephus, a Jew who defected to Rome after being captured during the revolt of AD 66–70, wrote that "God, who went the round of nations, bringing to each in turn the rod of empire, now rested over Italy."[4] Had the God of Israel switched allegiances?

JEWS DISPUTE THE LIMITS OF ACCOMMODATION TO PAGAN ROME

The Romans who controlled all the Mediterranean world in the first century worshiped many gods and were willing to recognize what they viewed as regional deities. Caesar Augustus began the practice of the Roman government funding a daily whole burnt offering "to the most high God" at the Jerusalem temple.[5] The sacrifice was not *to the emperor* as happened elsewhere in the Roman world. But that distinction did not satisfy devout Jews who feared that foreign influence would finally destroy their religion. When Jews began the great revolt against Rome in AD 66, their first move was to stop sacrifices on behalf of any foreigner.[6]

During Jesus' lifetime a series of Jewish freedom fighters tried unsuccessfully to throw off foreign rule. Herod the Great, a staunch ally of Rome, was wary of any such threat to his power and tried to kill the reputed "king of the Jews" born in Bethlehem (Matthew 2). About the time Jesus was born, a Jewish rebel named Judas and his followers attacked Sepphoris, administrative center of Herod the Great's rule in Galilee. Rebels made off with the regional government treasury and a quantity of weapons.[7] The book of Acts mentions two other failed rebellions (5:36–37), and there were more.[8]

JESUS PRESSES BEYOND BOUNDARIES AND FACES RESISTANCE

Amid such spiritual and political ferment, Jesus came announcing the kingdom of God for which many Jews longed. The proclamation was electrifying and drew crowds. Street demonstrators chanted "Blessed is the king who comes in the name of the Lord!" as Jesus entered Jerusalem for Passover week (Luke 19:38). That rallying cry seemed subversive to Romans and was polarizing for Jews. Jesus didn't look like the conquering messiah most Jews expected.

The early Jesus movement was almost entirely Jewish, but after the resurrection, Jesus told his followers to make disciples of "all nations" (or "all Gentiles" or "all foreigners"; see Matthew 28:19–20).[9] When persecution at Jerusalem scattered early believers, they began to carry out Jesus' global, cross-cultural mandate.

Philip brought news of the kingdom to Samaritans, then baptized an Ethiopian eunuch (Acts 8:4–40). As we have discussed, Peter baptized a Roman centurion at the Roman military base at Caesarea (Acts 10). Such spillover beyond ethnic boundaries was not the liberation of Israel that most Jews wanted. Jewish resistance to foreign influence eventually ignited full-scale revolt against Rome in AD 66. Jews who resisted changes in the application of Jewish law sometimes violently resisted early Christian evangelism.

CHRISTIANS DID NOT INTEND TO START A NEW RELIGION

Early Christian ambassadors did not see themselves as promoting a new religion. For them, Jesus was the Jewish messiah who unexpectedly and wonderfully opened a way for Gentiles to become children of Abraham. But when Christians began to reshape Judaism into what looked like a Jewish-Gentile religion, some Jews sensed that their spiritual heritage was under threat. An ardent young Jew named Saul, "breathing threats and murder" (Acts 9:1), got authorization from the high priest to arrest followers of Jesus at Damascus and bring them bound to Jerusalem.

A visionary encounter with the risen Christ stopped Saul in his tracks when he was on his way to Damascus. Persuaded that God was calling him through Jesus, Saul presented himself to the Christian community at Damascus for baptism. He began to use the Latin version of his name, Paul, appropriate for his conviction that he "had been entrusted with the task of preaching the gospel to the [Gentiles], just as Peter had been to the [Jews]" (Galatians 2:7 NIV).

Paul became convinced that humanity's restored relationship with God came as a gift through faith in the death and resurrection of Jesus, not through strict adherence to Jewish law. Though he called himself "blameless" in observing Jewish law (Philippians 3:6), Paul now saw obedience to God as an *outcome* of salvation rather than a means to attain it.

But Paul's view of obedience did not measure up to traditional Jewish understandings of observing Mosaic law. Notably, Paul did not teach Gentile believers the array of traditional Jewish purity rituals that most Pharisees considered indispensable. He did not even expect Gentile believers to practice circumcision, which for most Jews was nonnegotiable. The apostle seemed to ignore key scriptures, watering down Jewish faith by incorporating nonobservant Gentiles.

PAUL FACES THREATS FROM POLARIZED JEWS

Already at Damascus, where Paul first entered the Christian movement and began teaching in synagogues, he had to escape through a hole in the city wall because opponents wanted to kill him (Acts 9:23–25). Death threats continued when Paul got to Jerusalem (9:29) and followed as he set out across the Roman world to invite anyone who would listen to believe in the Jewish messiah.

As he traveled, Paul typically presented the message about Jesus first at Jewish synagogues. A repeating pattern emerges: Paul "argues" (or "discusses") in a synagogue, listeners become polarized, and opponents attack him (14:1–20; 18:1–17).[10] Frustrated by resistance to his message at Antioch in Pisidia (in modern-day Turkey), Paul told Jews at a synagogue there, "Since you reject [the word of God] and judge yourselves to be unworthy of eternal life, we are now turning to the Gentiles" (13:46).

THE RESURRECTION GIVES PAUL POWER FOR GLOBAL WITNESS

Resurrection was a central theme of Paul's mission work, and he sensed the risen Lord's presence. "I have been cruci-fied with Christ," he said, "and it is no longer I who live, but it is Christ who lives in me" (Galatians 2:19–20). Because of Jesus' resurrection, even Gentile believers had "clothed" themselves with Christ and become "Abraham's offspring, heirs according to the promise" (3:27–29). For Paul, deliv-ering that inclusive message led to imprisonment, flogging, stoning, sleepless nights, hunger, anxiety, and more (2 Corin-thians 11:23–28).

Missionaries who cross ethnic or cultural boundaries some-times make pastoral applications of the gospel that generate opposition in their own sending faith communities. Paul's sending community, which had close ties to the church in Jerusalem, was at Antioch. But his mission field was the entire Roman world. When Paul was arrested for the last time at the end of his public ministry, he was preparing to take the gospel westward to Spain, the far end of the Roman Empire. But before making that trek, he journeyed eastward to Jerusalem for what he called "a ministry to the saints" (see Romans 15:22–29). The apostle was so committed to the unity of the church that he would risk his life to build bridges across a bitter divide among followers of Jesus.

CRISIS CREATES OPPORTUNITY FOR RECONCILIATION

Jewish Christians at Jerusalem, many of whom did not welcome uncircumcised Gentiles, were in poverty when drought and famine ravaged Palestine in the AD 40s and 50s. Even before Paul began his mission journeys, a Christian prophet at Antioch "predicted by the Spirit that there would be a severe famine over all the world" (Acts 11:28). The famine was not global when it came, but it was severe in Jerusalem. Josephus says, "Many people died for want of what was necessary to procure food," prompting even Queen Helena of Adiabene (in present-day Iran) to send relief.[11] Christians at Antioch determined to collect an offering for believers in Jerusalem, and Paul helped carry the relief money there.

Years later, after Paul's mission outreach to Gentiles had caused bitter tension with conservative Jewish Christians at Jerusalem, the apostle helped organize a similar "ministry to the saints." This time the issue was not famine but poverty. Even though many in the church at Jerusalem probably considered Paul their most dangerous theological opponent, the apostle orchestrated a money gift for them from the largely Gentile congregations in Greece and Macedonia (Romans 15:22–33; 1 Corinthians 16:1–4; 2 Corinthians 8–9; Galatians 2:10). In his appeal to Gentile believers in those regions for generosity, Paul pointed to the example of Jesus. Jesus "was rich, yet for your sakes he became poor, so that by his poverty you might become rich" (2 Corinthians 8:9).

PAUL RISKS HIS LIFE TO REACH ACROSS THE DIVIDE

Paul and a small accountability group carried the Gentile relief money to Jerusalem. Paul wrote the book of Romans just before making that journey. He requested "earnest prayer to God on my behalf, that I may be rescued from the unbelievers in Judea" (Romans 15:30–31). Upon his arrival at Caesarea in Palestine, Christian friends there implored him not to risk making the final ascent up to Jerusalem. To make sure Paul got the point, a Christian prophet bound his own feet and hands to show what opponents at Jerusalem would do to the apostle. "I am ready not only to be bound," Paul declared, "but even to die in Jerusalem for the name of the Lord Jesus" (Acts 21:13).

The apostle initially got a warm reception from senior church leaders when he arrived at Jerusalem, but trouble was brewing. Paul's opponents at Jerusalem included not only traditional Jews, but *thousands* of Jewish followers of Jesus who were "zealous for the law" (Acts 21:20). This reflected serious division in the early Christian movement. Jewish Christians believed that Paul was teaching people "to forsake Moses" (21:21).

That is not how Paul would have described his relationship to the Torah, but it was enough to generate a rumor that he had desecrated the temple by bringing a ritually unfit Gentile into it. A lynch mob dragged Paul out of the temple precinct, and only swift intervention by Roman soldiers spared him from death.

Roman soldiers saved Paul at Jerusalem, but he spent more than two years in prison at Caesarea on the Mediterranean coast before being transferred to Rome for two more years of house arrest (Acts 28:16, 30–31). The apostle then disappears from history, and we have no certain account of how he died. Clement of Rome wrote late in the first century that Paul succeeded in preaching the gospel to "the farthest limits of the West," possibly meaning Spain.[12] If indeed Paul went to Spain, it presumably would have been after his two-year house arrest at Rome. In any case, the apostle likely died in Rome along with Peter and other believers when Emperor Nero falsely accused Christians of having started the great fire that destroyed much of the city in AD 64.[13]

GOD MAY WELCOME EVEN THOSE WITH WHOM WE DISAGREE

Paul was at Corinth, halfway between Rome and Jerusalem, when he wrote the book of Romans. He sent the epistle westward to the imperial capital, then headed eastward to Jerusalem where he braced for opposition. When we consider that an approaching encounter with harsh critics at Jerusalem was on the apostle's mind, phrases scattered throughout Romans 12–15 are poignant: "We, who are many, are one body in Christ. . . . Live in harmony with one another. . . . Love is the fulfilling of the law. . . . No longer pass judgment on one another. . . . Welcome one another . . ."

Amid these exhortations to forbearance, the apostle briefly addresses a specific controversy that strained relations between Jewish Christians and Gentile converts: dietary regulations. The Law of Moses included strict instructions for what meat was permissible and how it was to be prepared. On top of these concerns was the vexing reality that much meat in public markets had been "sacrificed to idols" (1 Corinthians 8:1). A portion of the slaughtered animals was used for sacrifice at pagan temples and the rest sold to the public.

Given these complications, some Christians were vegetarian. Others argued that since pagan gods were not real, it would not matter if a portion of meat had been used in sacrifice (8:4). Paul counseled the church at Rome,

> Those who eat must not despise those who abstain, and those who abstain must not pass judgment on those who eat; for God has welcomed them. Who are you to pass judgment on servants of another? (Romans 14:3–4)

In a divided church, Christians should be slow to judge or condemn. God welcomes fellow believers, even those with whom we may have disputes, and we should err on the side of grace. Paul was ready to lay down his life to show love toward persons who sometimes angered him. He came to see that unity of the church was more important than unanimity, and *without compromising his conviction* made the costly trip to Jerusalem for reconciliation.

AMID SEXUALITY DEBATES WE STILL RESPECT EACH OTHER

Today's ecclesial disputes about sexuality seem more complicated than early church disagreements about diet. Sexual orientation is not a matter of conscious choice but of deep-seated personal identity. Nevertheless, what Paul counsels in addressing concerns about diet is relevant for us today: "If your brother or sister is being injured by what you eat, you are no longer walking in love" (Romans 14:15).

If we apply this pastoral insight to sexuality debates, it must not mean that we push people into secrecy about their identity. But it might mean that congregations or denominations debating policy on sexuality will refrain from making categorical pronouncements that effectively excommunicate one side or the other. Loving, God-fearing, faithful Christians will continue to bring scripture and experience to bear on a matter that remains disputed.

I was raised in a denomination that categorically rejected any expression of same-sex attraction. Today, parts of my denomination have changed. There now are some who take a rigidly *progressive* stance on LGBTQ matters, insisting that the church, including those who are conservative, apologize for their understandings of sexuality in the past or present. Christians in fact have often grievously harmed gay and lesbian people over the centuries, and the church should acknowledge that. But we would do well to consider the wisdom of Dan Leatherman of Colorado, who came out as gay four decades ago. He faced the "inevitable ostracism," and today says,

> Knowing what it's like to be part of a minority, I want to be gracious enough to include those who differ with me in biblical interpretation. Most "anti-gay" Mennonites are not mean-spirited bigots; they sincerely believe progressives are promoting deeply sinful behavior. To insist [that conservatives] repent seems like forcing an innocent person to falsely confess in a plea bargain. When both sides claim the moral high ground, separation seems inevitable. What saddens me are the broken relationships.[14]

I yearn for divided or fractured denominations to model that kind of love and respect. Could leaders of separated church bodies attend the other group's annual sessions and perhaps bring greetings? Could leaders periodically meet, not to rehash old arguments but to learn what God is doing in another part of the body of Christ? Are there service projects that could bring members of separated groups together? Could we have joint hymn sings? "Welcome one another . . .

just as Christ has welcomed you," Paul tells disputing factions within the church at Rome (Romans 15:7).

It is important for believers in today's conflicted church to recognize that unity was a struggle from the beginning of the Christian movement. As New Testament scholar Paul Achtemeier says,

> Unless we are aware of the problems the early church faced concerning its unity, we will inevitably romanticize that period and either give up in despair at the course taken by subsequent developments in the history of the church, or else assume in a naive way that all it takes to recover that lost, original unity is a little good will and some pleasant negotiations.[15]

Accepting that reality, however, must not stop us from demonstrating the love of Jesus toward people who differ from us.

Chapter 8
REFLECT AND DISCUSS

1. Tell the story of someone you know or admire who took risks to cross religious, political, or social polarities for the sake of the gospel. What price did they pay? What was gained?

2. When have you seen tension or contrasting beliefs develop between a mission church and its parent congregation or denomination? How would you explain that polarity? Was it ever resolved?

3. What happens today when there are acts of generosity between churches who disagree with each other? Have you or someone you know reached across such a divide? How was that act received? Do you recommend such action?

4. What is the difference between unity and unanimity in your experience of church? Can you think of examples?

5. What questions does this chapter raise for you?

RIGHT REMEMBERING FOSTERS HEALING

I humbly beg forgiveness for the evil committed by so many Christians against the Indigenous peoples," Pope Francis declared before a large crowd of Indigenous people during a 2022 visit to Alberta.[1] With that apology, the Catholic Church joined the Canadian government and Protestant churches of Canada to acknowledge the catastrophic physical, sexual, and cultural abuse suffered by 150,000 Indigenous children who were forced into residential schools across Canada between 1870 and 1996.

Recent radar scans at the former schools—many administered by churches—revealed hundreds of unmarked graves, believed to belong to children who perished in the project to erase Indigenous identity. The United States has its own sordid history of residential school abuse, part of a larger pattern of domination that alienated Native peoples from mainstream American society. Land theft, racial prejudice, and genocide have made relations between European immigrants and Indigenous peoples one of the most excruciating polarities of the modern era.

A CHEYENNE CHIEF WELCOMES US TO HIS HOME

Cheyenne peace chief Lawrence Hart gave a broad smile and a warm handshake when my wife Ellen and I entered his living room in Oklahoma. Because eighty-eight-year-old Hart was physically limited and not speaking much, his wife Betty did most of the talking about their boundary-crossing lives. On the wall of their living room was a photograph of Hart's grandfather John P. Hart in full ceremonial attire of a Cheyenne chief.

Hart's grandfather had been sent as a child from Oklahoma to be "civilized" at the Carlisle Indian Industrial School in Pennsylvania, the first boarding school in the United States for Indigenous children. Students there had to abandon Native language and customs as they prepared to assimilate into White American culture. "Kill the Indian, save the man" was the mantra of the Carlisle school, which became a model for hundreds of similar institutions.

But John P. Hart did not abandon his cultural heritage. He returned to Oklahoma, where he became a tribal chief and joined the Native American Church, which blended Cheyenne traditions with Christian faith. Now Ellen and I were visiting his grandson, hoping we could do "right remembering."

I first heard that term in 2004 when Lutherans and Mennonites jointly acknowledged painful past relations between the two denominations and committed to an amicable future (see ch. 11). Right remembering means to acknowledge wrongs we did to others in the past while also committing to positive relations with them going forward. Asking to meet Chief Hart and his wife was a small step my wife and I could take in our effort to understand how European settlers and Indigenous people interacted in American history.

MY IMAGE OF INDIGENOUS HISTORY WAS ROMANTICIZED

On the farm where I was born in eastern Pennsylvania my family found Native American arrowheads that conjured romantic images for me as a child. Native Americans had once hunted there with bow and arrow! It did not occur to me that those people were victims of ethnic cleansing, or even that they had provided local place-names such as Susquehanna and Conestoga. I had no sense that tragedy overtook them when my Mennonite ancestors colonized Lancaster County.

In George Orwell's novel *1984*, totalitarian rulers of a dystopian society repeat the phrase "Who controls the past controls the future: who controls the present controls the past." The governing party in Orwell's novel rewrote history to make it say what they wanted so history would seem to justify what they were doing in the present.

There are people who sanitize American history as well, especially as taught in public schools. If schools teach about slavery or the history of racial discrimination, parents and politicians sometimes accuse them of promoting critical race theory, or CRT. Critical race theory premises that racism, rooted in a long history of discrimination, continues to distort political, economic, and social structures of society today. Critical race theory is primarily an academic discipline relegated to higher education, and there is little evidence that K–12 students are exposed to it. But those who oppose teaching in the schools about racism or discrimination prefer that youth learn idealized narratives of American history, not sins of the past that may require acknowledgment or reparations.

But how can White persons like me make sense of racial and ethnic polarization in the United States today without knowing something of the realities of slavery, Jim Crow laws,

disenfranchisement, dispossession, lynchings, discriminatory policing, and other forms of injustice that have shaped
American society? How can we understand the challenges
and alienation that Indigenous peoples face today if we don't
know their stories and the story of their land on which we
now live?

WE TAKE A ROAD TRIP TO LEARN ABOUT INDIGENOUS CULTURE AND HISTORY

In 2021, Ellen and I towed a pop-up camper from our home
in Indiana to where our daughter lives in California. To learn
more about Indigenous people, we visited Native American
historical sites in Oklahoma, Utah, Arizona, New Mexico,
Colorado, and California. We tried to broaden our understanding of American history by reading *Bury My Heart at
Wounded Knee* and *An Indigenous People's History of the
United States*. Native American museums, art galleries, and
archeological sites filled our senses with cultural riches. We
hiked through canyons to see ancient Indigenous rock art.

While driving round-trip to California, we read aloud
Robin Wall Kimmerer's award-winning book *Braiding Sweet-
grass: Indigenous Wisdom, Scientific Knowledge, and the
Teachings of Plants*. An enrolled member of the Potawatomi
Nation, Kimmerer is a professor of environmental and for-
est biology in upstate New York. Director of the Center for
Native Peoples and the Environment, she blends traditional
Indigenous ecological wisdom with modern Western biology
to promote reciprocal and sustainable models of relationship
with the natural world.

Kimmerer occasionally draws from an Indigenous creation story about Skywoman, who came from Skyworld to
a flooded earth and found rest only on the back of a turtle.

Turtle Island—which some traditions use to refer to Earth, others to the continent of North America—emerged from that meeting of sky and earth. Kimmerer writes,

> The earth was new then, when it welcomed the first human. It's old now, and some suspect that we have worn out our welcome by casting the Original Instructions aside. From the very beginning of the world, the other species were a lifeboat for the people. Now, we must be theirs. But the stories that might guide us, if they are told at all, grow dim in the memory. . . . Skywoman seems to look me in the eye and ask, in return for this gift of a world on Turtle's back, what will I give in return?[2]

Today, with climate change accelerating and nuclear threat on the horizon, it is both chastening and inspiring to hear how Indigenous peoples have lived in reciprocal relationship with the natural world. Kimmerer briefly touches on some associations between Native stories and Christian faith, but Ellen and I made further connections. The biblical creation account similarly begins with water covering the face of the earth, and the book of Genesis also shows humanity losing the Original Instructions.

CHIEF HART COMMITS HIS LIFE TO THE GOSPEL OF PEACE

Learning about the life of Cheyenne chief Lawrence Hart helped us understand more of the Native experience in America.[3] Hart was largely raised by his grandparents, who practiced traditional Cheyenne customs but also had close association with a Mennonite mission church. That intersection of Cheyenne culture and Christian faith set direction for Lawrence's life. He chose to follow Christ at age seventeen and for two years attended Bethel College, a Mennonite school in Kansas.

Then he enlisted in the US Air Force and was one of the first Native Americans to become a fighter pilot.

When his grandfather died in 1958 while Lawrence was in the military, tribal leaders asked Lawrence to succeed him in tribal leadership. Like his grandfather, Lawrence would be a peace chief fostering good relations within and beyond the tribe. Accepting the call, Lawrence piloted an air force jet from Texas to Oklahoma, smoked the peace pipe in a teepee with tribal elders, and became a leader of his people. On his solo flight back to Texas, Chief Hart got permission to detour over the Gulf of Mexico. There he soared to great height, put the aircraft into a steep dive, and broke the sound barrier.[4]

I asked Chief Hart in 2021 which of his piloting memories was most vivid. Without speaking he swept his index finger across in front him and up into a large, slow loop—then grinned. But though he loved flying, both his position as peace chief and his early pacifist, Mennonite formation meant he would abandon his air force career. Lawrence completed his commissioned time of military service, finished a degree at Bethel College in Kansas, and became a minister. He would spend the rest of his life working for peace both as a tribal leader and as a minister of the gospel.

OKLAHOMA CITY BOMBING RECALLS THE SLAUGHTER OF INDIGENOUS PEOPLE

Chief Hart's legacy in those roles is storied. From 1963 to 2021 he served as pastor of Koinonia Mennonite Church in Clinton, Oklahoma. He established a Cheyenne cultural center nearby and worked nationally to inter bones of Native people that were on display in museums. Twice Chief Hart appeared before a subcommittee of the US Congress in support of making a national memorial site along the Washita River in Oklahoma where Cheyenne people were massacred.

The first request failed, but Congress called him to testify a second time shortly after the 1995 Oklahoma City bombing that killed 168 persons. There was discussion at the time of making the Oklahoma City site a national memorial park. Chief Hart told a congressional committee, "The site in Oklahoma City is hallowed ground just as the site where the [Cheyenne] village stood at Washita." Congress was persuaded, and today the Washita Battlefield National Historic Site is administered by the National Park Service.

Ellen and I had visited the Oklahoma City National Memorial as we came through the state. A serene reflecting pool marks the place where an anti-government terrorist bomb destroyed the Alfred P. Murrah Federal Building. Next to the pool is the Field of Empty Chairs with 168 sculptured seats in neat rows, one for each victim. Nineteen small chairs represent children who perished.

The perpetrators of this massacre were White supremacists who hated centralized government, and their crime traumatized the nation. In comparison, it is impossible to know exactly how many massacres of Indigenous people have been committed in North America, but they number in the *hundreds*. Chief Hart was right: American people must never forget these places where polarization led to hatred and death.

Though Chief Hart spoke little when Ellen and I visited, we asked if he and Betty would sing in Cheyenne. In strong voice and joyful tones, he and Betty sang the hymn "Jesus, Nahoonòsetano" ("Jesus, I Am Lonesome"). The song speaks to Jesus of being lonesome and longing to go home to heaven where relatives have already gone.[5]

Chief Hart went home ten months after singing this lament. Before we left him, he filled the room with a heartfelt prayer in Cheyenne. We understood none of the words, but praise and blessing came through clearly. We also blessed the Harts, then went on our way to the Washita Battlefield. At that place, in 1868, Lt. Col. George Armstrong Custer had commanded the 7th US Cavalry in a surprise attack on a Cheyenne encampment that was under the leadership of Peace Chief Black Kettle.

PEACE CHIEF BLACK KETTLE AND HIS PEOPLE DIE AT WASHITA

The history of the Washita Battlefield is one chapter in a long saga of colonial betrayals. Chief Black Kettle tried to build good relations with encroaching European settlers at a time when government policy was edging toward annihilation of Native peoples. Because of Chief Black Kettle's efforts to establish peace with White settlers, the band was ostracized by other Native peoples and pushed out of the relative safety of the larger Cheyenne community.

Custer and his troops attacked Black Kettle and his band without warning while they were most vulnerable, on a bitterly cold winter morning in 1868. Some Cheyenne—including armed men from nearby Cheyenne camps who rushed to the scene—returned fire, killing nineteen of Custer's men. Peace Chief Black Kettle and his wife Medicine Woman did not fight, but as they fled both were shot in the back and died. Inflating his account, Custer bragged that his troops killed 103 "warriors." The toll almost certainly was fewer but included many women and children. Custer's soldiers also corralled and slaughtered 675 ponies, animals essential for the people's survival on the prairies.

Ellen and I spent two hours in utter solitude at that killing field. The rolling grasslands are evocative, and prairie wind was the only sound. We soaked up the stillness and prayed at the river crossing where Black Kettle and Medicine Woman died. Chief Lawrence Hart's great-grandmother Afraid of Beavers survived the massacre. She was a sister of Medicine Woman and was in the group who searched for and found the bodies of the chief and his wife.[6]

WRONG REMEMBERING CAN DAMAGE A COMMUNITY

Chief Lawrence Hart was startled in 1968 when the chamber of commerce of a nearby town decided to reenact the Washita battle on its hundredth anniversary. Town officials had the audacity to ask Indigenous people to play the part of Chief Black Kettle and his band. Tribal leaders reluctantly agreed to participate on condition that the reenactment be historically accurate and events of the day include interment of the remains of a Cheyenne victim that had been on display at a museum.

Unbeknownst to Cheyenne people who participated in the reenactment, a group calling themselves "Grandsons" of Custer's regiment planned to participate. At the fateful anniversary hour, on the site of the 1868 massacre, Grandsons of Custer in replica uniforms charged over a nearby hilltop on horseback. Their guns blazed with blank cartridges while their loudspeaker played "Garryowen," traditional marching tune of the 7th US Cavalry.

The reenactment was too real, and it terrified Cheyenne participants. Chief Hart was furious, and his first impulse was to avoid any further interaction with the Grandsons. But to his dismay, they showed up later that day at the solemn procession to bury remains of an 1868 massacre victim. The Grandsons respectfully stood at attention. As part of the ceremony, a handmade wool blanket covering the interment box would be given to some worthy person among the attendees—perhaps the governor of Oklahoma.

But when Lawrence consulted with other chiefs, they chose to bequeath the blanket to the captain of Custer's "Grandsons." At the public ceremony, Lawrence called the captain to the podium and the blanket was wrapped around the man's shoulders. "People broke down and cried," Lawrence later recalled. "We too cried on each other's shoulders—these grandsons of the Seventh and grandsons of Black Kettle." The captain removed the Garry Owen regimental pin from his uniform, gave it to Chief Hart, and pledged, "Never again will your people hear 'Garryowen.'"[7]

MOSES TEACHES RIGHT REMEMBERING

Just before Israelites crossed the Jordan River to settle in Canaan, Moses instructed them to remember rightly so they would act justly:

> You shall not deprive a resident alien or an orphan of justice; you shall not take a widow's garment in pledge. Remember that you were a slave in Egypt and the LORD your God redeemed you from there. . . . When you gather the grapes of your vineyard, do not glean what is left; it shall be for the alien, the orphan, and the widow. Remember that you were a slave in the land of Egypt; therefore I am commanding you to do this. (Deuteronomy 24:17–22)

I wish Moses had said, "Remember never to slaughter the Canaanites." I have trouble reconciling powerful themes of social justice in the Torah with the command to conquer and annihilate. That remains an unresolved biblical polarity for me (but see earlier discussion of genocide in chapter 2).

I cannot take responsibility for what ancient Israelites understood God to command, but I can work for justice in my homeland. My ancestors have been in North America since colonial days, and Moses might say, *Remember that you were an immigrant in this country.* Remember that Indiana, land on which you live, was cherished by Potawatomi people who were forced from their homes to distant reservations and is cherished today by their descendants.

AN IMMIGRANT FAMILY MAKES REPARATIONS

When Florence Schloneger inherited a portion of the family farm in Kansas where she was raised, she wanted to do more than simply remember injustices of the past. She wanted to take some meaningful step of restitution to Kansa (Kaw) people from whom the property was taken in the nineteenth century. Schloneger is a Mennonite minister, and her ancestors were among eighteen thousand Mennonites who migrated from Ukraine to the American Great Plains starting in the 1870s. Those immigrants came because of Russian military conscription and state control of their schools.

The Russian migration part of Schloneger's story gets my attention since my home congregation in Elkhart, Indiana, hosted many of those immigrants as they passed through our city on the railroad. The founding pastor of my congregation, John Funk, even traveled to the Great Plains to help scout out "available" land for fellow Mennonites to purchase. Arrival of those pacifist settlers often came on the heels of betrayal and massacre committed by others.

When Chief Lawrence Hart and other religious leaders launched a nationwide "Return to the Earth" project to give dignified burial to Native American remains kept at museums, Pastor Schloneger got involved. Along with other Mennonite and Amish craftsmen, people from her congregation built small cedar boxes for the burials. She learned all she could about the Kansa people who had been forcibly removed a few years before her great-great-grandparents arrived as homesteaders in Kansas in 1879.

A fifth-generation settler, Schloneger was raised on that homestead farm. Her forebears did not personally use force of arms, but that made little difference to displaced Indigenous people. "My Mennonite ancestors settled in Pennsylvania, Virginia, Ohio, Illinois, Nebraska, and Kansas," she said, "and in every case they moved in as homesteaders within five years of Native people being forced out."[8]

Schloneger looked for a way to return at least a portion ($10,000) of the proceeds from the sale of her farmland inheritance to Kansa (Kaw) people. She contacted Pauline Sharp, a member of the Kaw Nation who served as vice president of the Kaw Nation Cultural Committee. "There were a lot of tears at that meeting," Schloneger recalled, "my tears for what my ancestors had done; Pauline Sharp's tears that someone recognized injustices done to her people."

INDIGENOUS PEOPLE NAME WHAT THEY HAVE LOST

Kansa people had never before received a reparation payment, and with Schloneger's funds they formed the Kansa Heritage Society. Sharp and Schloneger became friends, and soon received invitations to tell their respective ancestral stories together. Sharp's presentation included this account:

> Prior to 1825, the Kaw domain was 20 million acres. A series of treaties reduced their land to 2 million, to 256,000, then to 80,000 acres. . . .

European contact and settlement meant disease and the loss of hunting grounds. By 1873 there were 533 Kaw people left who were forced to go to Indian Territory [Oklahoma], a trek of seventeen days and 165 miles. When they arrived, no provisions had been made for them. Soon many more died of typhoid, malnutrition, and starvation. The elders thought they had been sent to Indian Territory to die, so they gave away all their sacred objects. During this time, my grandmother was born in a tipi on the banks of Little Beaver Creek.[9]

Schloneger's brother Ken Rodgers also gave $10,000, and now matches whatever he pays in property taxes annually as an additional payment to the Kansa. Schloneger does not think she and her brother have done anything heroic. "It's a small step," she said. She does not think of the money as a gift; it is "symbolic reparation."[10]

GET IN TOUCH WITH YOUR OWN HISTORY

The first step immigrant descendants should take, Schloneger says, is to "get in touch with your own history. What Native peoples were on your land? How do you benefit from what was taken from them?"[11] Few settler families in North America are doing as much as Schloneger and her brother to address sins against Indigenous peoples. But what might appear relatively generous to some persons of European descent still looks woefully inadequate to Native Americans. George Tinker, a Lutheran pastor and elder from the Osage Nation, spoke these words in 2015 when a Lutheran congregation in Colorado returned a piece of property to Native people via the Four Winds American Indian Council:

Christians like to talk about reconciliation . . . *re-concile*, to concile again. And Indians won't have it. We aren't conciled, we were never conciled. We were pushed and pushed out of our lands, our people killed, our cultures and languages destroyed. When they talk about reconciliation, what Christians are really saying is, "Can you forgive us for when we took the land?" The bottom line is, "Can we keep the land in good conscience?"

So "reconciliation" is not about the Indians, but about the guilt Christians feel. Sorry, it's not that easy. Our job is not to make you feel good. After you committed mass genocide, the only possible reparation is land.[12]

These are hard words to hear. I confess that my mind starts making excuses. At least some of my Mennonite ancestors in Europe were hounded off their land by persecutors centuries ago; should I expect reparations? What about the sometimes harmful interactions between Indigenous groups before my ancestors arrived in America?

DO SOMETHING IN RESPONSE TO INJUSTICES OF THE PAST

Whataboutism is an inadequate response to ethical issues because it's a way to avoid responsibility. Malefactors in Europe may have done wrong to my forebears, and Indigenous groups may have harmed each other. But that has nothing to do with ethical choices I make now about land I own that was taken from Potawatomi people.[13]

It is easy to feel overwhelmed by injustices of history, but it is important for people like me to do *something* in response. We can start by learning about the past, acknowledging that wrongs done by our forebears created privileges that we enjoy today. We can declare with the Hebrew psalmist, "Both we and our ancestors have sinned; we have committed iniquity, have done wickedly" (Psalm 106:6).

Rather than seeking *reconciliation* with Indigenous people, we can work at *conciliation*—taking initiatives of respect and justice, attending a powwow or other gathering (at the invitation of its hosts, of course), supporting organizations that promote Indigenous cultures. Educating ourselves about the past can start a journey that leads to greater things such as returning land or including Indigenous tribes or other groups in estate planning. We should not expect Indigenous people to forgive all injustices of the past, or even to take time to be our friends. But they are right to expect people like me to act justly now.

Chapter 9

REFLECT AND DISCUSS

1. What do you know about people who occupied land where you live before the arrival of Europeans? Have you built any relationships with Indigenous survivors? Do you know anyone who has apologized for the past or made reparations?

2. What impressions of Indigenous peoples have you gotten through television, movies, books, or popular culture? If those impressions were unfair, where do you turn for a reliable picture of past and present Indigenous people?

3. If you have visited Indigenous communities, museums, or historical sites, how did that change your view of Native people and immigrants?

4. How has the debate over critical race theory affected schools or other entities in your area? What do you think should be the function of history in schools and churches, especially in relation to injustices of the past?

5. What questions does this chapter raise for you?

SYSTEMIC RACISM SHAPED MY NEIGHBORHOOD

Two days before Christmas of 2013, an altercation flared among three Black teenagers in a car behind Prairie Street Mennonite Church in Elkhart, Indiana, where I served on the pastoral team. Money and drugs were at issue. The dispute ended with one young man firing a revolver, killing eighteen-year-old Devonte "Ray" Patrick.[1] Events after this tragedy would teach me about polarization between Black and White people in American society.

Few people in our congregation knew Devonte Ray. But how, we asked, could we celebrate the birth of Jesus on Christmas Eve just one day after such violence? With the Christmas Eve program already planned, the pastoral team decided to have our usual joyous service at five in the evening. Then at six o'clock we would gather in the parking lot for a candlelight vigil to grieve and pray.

Unbeknownst to us, a local television station incorrectly announced that the vigil for Devonte Ray would be at five o'clock, not six. When our mostly White congregation came for the nativity celebration at five, forty Black neighbors also streamed into the sanctuary. It was a perfect storm of miscommunication. People prepared to sing "Joy to the World" filled the front half of the auditorium. Grieving neighbors, including young friends of Devonte Ray, filled the back. Devante Ray's mother Angela Tanner sat dazed and devastated, surrounded by family.

The rear of the congregation soon became restless with stage-whisper comments as the celebration got underway. One young man finally blurted angrily for all to hear, "This is supposed to be about Devonte! Why are we being happy?" I wish I or someone at the church had intervened at that point, spoken to the whole group, and changed the course of the gathering. But not understanding what had been miscommunicated, we let the program continue.

When the service ended, everyone processed silently out into the winter chill. Black and White participants carried candles and huddled around the tragedy site. There was silence, scripture reading, prayer, and tears. Then everyone came in from the cold for hot chocolate in the fellowship hall. The Black mourners mostly just wanted to talk with each other. But there were also courteous, if stilted, conversations between the two groups.

TRAGEDY BRINGS AN ASSIGNMENT

I felt shattered. On top of the unbearable sadness of a youth dying on our property, the congregation had inflicted further pain on the Black community by celebrating in their presence when they were in shock. A week after the vigil, I went to the nearby home of Devonte Ray's mother. To my surprise she greeted me warmly and invited me in to visit with her and her mother.

What I did not know was that God was at work in Angela Tanner's life. In later conversation she told me that on the day Devonte Ray died she came home from the hospital "and cried and cried until I could not cry anymore." Her life had derailed in part because of her own struggles with alcohol and drug abuse, and she pleaded to God for salvation. "I felt God wrap his arms around me," she recalled. "I felt the love of Christ. I said, 'Normal mothers do not bury their children. Something has to change.' I gave my life to Jesus—and knew at that moment that God had given me an assignment. I never went back to the dope house or liquor store again."

An assignment. Angela Tanner was determined not to let her son's death be a waste. Each subsequent December 23 on the anniversary of the tragedy, Prairie Street Church joined her and others from Elkhart for a candlelight vigil at the place where Devonte Ray died. We read aloud the names of people—provided to us by the police department—who had died from gun violence in our city during the previous year. Then we gathered in the church to hear speakers from organizations countering gun violence. The local press reported these events and amplified our call for gun control.

RAY OF HOPE SUPPORTS FORMER PRISONERS AND FAMILIES OF VICTIMS

The assignment was always on Angela Tanner's mind. She began to talk about her dream of reaching out to young men who were finding their way in society after prison. The idea came from what happened when she attended the trials of the two accused of slaying her son: "I noticed that one of the young men convicted for killing my son never had one person come to support him. That was almost as heartbreaking as losing my son. I began to wonder how I could help young men or women like that who need to find a moral compass, hope, and a vision for their future."[2]

Her brother Adrian Riley, a committed Christian who worked as a counselor at the county jail, joined his sister to form Ray of Hope Foundation. Their vision is "to give youth and adults the opportunity to become successful citizens by providing families with the tools and resources needed to produce a safe, healthy, and stable environment for emotional, physical, and mental stability."[3]

Ray of Hope Foundation created a support group for persons who had lost a family member to gun violence. Angela Tanner and her brother sought training and set up a program to provide counsel to help others make responsible life decisions.[4] Local judges began referring men coming out of prison to their program.

Prairie Street Church erected a simple stone boulder with a plaque at the place where Devonte Ray died. In a surprise of God's grace that I never could have anticipated, Angela Tanner now runs Ray of Hope from an office in the church basement. She and Adrian provide classes for men who are adjusting to life outside of prison. On Sundays, this sister and brother lead a Bible study in their homes with men recently released.

A BLACK MAN EXTENDS MERCY TO WHITE SUPREMACISTS

Adrian Riley described what it was like as a Black man to show mercy even to White supremacists who were assigned to attend life skills classes he taught at the county jail. "There's a difference between mercy and forgiveness," he told me. "Mercy is when you treat a person as if they asked for forgiveness; forgiveness is what you do when they actually ask. I didn't treat the Aryan Nation men any different, and didn't judge what they believe," Adrian recalled. "I just said, 'I'm here to help you.' It takes love to break through, and occasionally one of the guys would come back and say I had changed his mind about Black people."

Aryan Nation men in prison sometimes attended Adrian's Bible study, which he called the Perfect Law of Liberty. The name comes from James 1:23–25:

> If any are hearers of the word and not doers, they are like those who look at themselves in a mirror; for they look at themselves and, on going away, immediately forget what they were like. But those who look into the perfect law, the law of liberty, and persevere, being not hearers who forget but doers who act—they will be blessed in their doing.

Adrian tried to get all participants to take a hard look at themselves. He urged White men not simply to blame people of another race for their problems and urged Black men not simply to blame racism. Taking responsibility for their own lives would free them to move forward as productive members of society.

Adrian now serves as the community liaison for the Elkhart Police Department. He fosters communication between law enforcement and multiethnic neighborhoods where—as in many American communities—there have been charges of racial profiling. His friendships constantly cross racial and cultural lines, and he cites Isaiah 1:18 as a vocational theme: "Come now, and let us reason together, saith the LORD: though your sins be as scarlet, they shall be as white as snow; though they be red like crimson, they shall be as wool" (KJV).

That verse is particularly fitting in a neighborhood where young men sometimes kill each other, where residents sometimes die from law enforcement bullets, where streets sometimes turn crimson. Isaiah's summons to "reason together" follows immediately on verses 15 and 17: "Your hands are full of blood. . . . Learn to do good; seek justice, rescue the oppressed . . ."

RACISM DISADVANTAGES THE BLACK COMMUNITY

Because of how American society has functioned over the centuries, Black people today face disproportionately high mortality rates and are more likely to experience violence, including from law enforcement. The school-to-prison pipeline leads to a disproportionate number of Black people in prison, especially young men.[5] And Black people often do not have access to affordable housing or to generational wealth through home ownership. These are just a few of the ways that structural racism disadvantages the Black community.

As a White person, it is tempting to say that these problems are not my fault. I'm not a racist, I like to think. But even if the past is not my fault, as a White person I benefit socially, politically, and economically from long-established patterns of the world around me. Persons of loving intention can benefit from *systems* that disadvantage others. Financial systems, schools, churches, employers, and political networks function in ways that give me, an educated White male, advantages that people in other sectors of society do not enjoy.

Women, Black people, and poor people have been saying this for generations. Ironically, my status and privilege as a White male makes it more likely that my message will be heard. That is reason for me to support less privileged voices, especially as I recognize that I have not borne the pain from which these insights emerged.

A BLACK LIVES MATTER SIGN ELICITS CONVERSATION

Like millions around the world, my wife and I were haunted by images of George Floyd dying under the knee of a callous policeman in 2020. We got a Black Lives Matter sign and perched it on our lawn at a place where it would be hard for a passing vehicle to run down. The sign went up even though a retired policeman lives directly across the street. No one flattened our sign, but it generated conversation.

The first exchange was with a Black woman who stopped her car on the street when my wife and I were doing lawn work. She asked, "Where did you get that sign? I need one of those!" We named the source, and her whole being communicated gratitude. Did our simple act of solidarity make some small difference in her life?

The second conversation was with a ten-year-old Black boy who lives with a White foster family on our street. I have not met his foster family, but I know little Reuben[6] because he cruises our subdivision on his bicycle. He knows that I am impressed with his wheelie-popping talent, so he rides circles around me and performs stunts when I walk for exercise. He is eager to talk and was by my side when we came by the Black Lives Matter sign.

"Why do you have that sign?" Reuben asked with a hint of suspicion. Was he curious about the meaning of the sign or about the fact that a White guy put it up? "Because too often when police think a Black man possibly did something wrong," I said, "the Black man gets hurt or even killed. That doesn't happen as often to White men. Black lives should matter as much as White lives."

Reuben pondered these words, pedaled slowly in silence, then said something unexpected: "You must have a very good father." I felt a flood of emotion. What experience in the life of this child had generated that comment? "Yes," I said, "I have a good father. He's ninety-eight." Wide-eyed, Reuben exclaimed, "*Ninety-eight!*" Then he popped another wheelie and rode off.

SYSTEMIC RACISM SHAPED MY NEIGHBORHOOD

Things were more complicated in the third conversation, with retired policeman Jesse Carter,[7] who lives across the street from our home. Former officer Carter is not quick to talk about himself, but our exchange was especially interesting because he is Black. When he and I met at our mailboxes not long after George Floyd's death, I said I had two things I wanted to tell him: I'm glad we are neighbors, and I grieve what happens to Black men in this country.

Carter thought for a minute and said, "What was that policeman *thinking*? That's not how you make an arrest. What was he *thinking*?" Then, pushing beyond his usual reserve, Carter responded to my comment about us being neighbors. "When I wanted to buy a lot in this neighborhood in 1973," he said, "the developer wouldn't sell to a Black person." That comment jolted me, even though my neighbor was chuckling when he said it.

I learned that the lot where Carter now lives was first purchased by a White family. When those owners decided not to build, Carter bought the land from them. Is he bitter about what happened half a century ago? "No," he said, laughing again. "That's just the way things *were*."

At least until the passage of the Fair Housing Act in 1968, it was common for American towns and cities to "redline" a portion of urban maps. This discriminatory practice targeted neighborhoods with significant numbers of racial and ethnic minorities and low-income residents. During the Great Migration from the South, which began in the 1910s and lasted through the midcentury, Black Americans who moved to the North, Midwest, and West often found housing in low-rent urban areas. Banks often redlined those areas of the city map, declaring mortgages there to be high risk. Property values tanked in those parts of town.

The Fair Housing Act also addressed another discriminatory practice: racial covenants. These were clauses in deeds of sale indicating that the property could never be sold to or occupied by Black people. Although the Fair Housing Act made such covenants illegal, they often still functioned in practice.

Officer Carter told me that when he was doing finish work on his house in 1973, a neighbor stopped by and said suspiciously, "Why do you want to live here?" I knew that neighbor, now deceased. He was an ardent lay evangelist who could impart the Christian plan of salvation to anyone who would listen. I did not resonate with his concept of salvation. But to his credit, years after asking that racist question, the man came back to apologize.

That story reflects just one facet of White supremacy that Black people have experienced in this country. My Swiss forebears came to America voluntarily in the mid-eighteenth century, not in chains like the ancestors of many Black Americans.[8] I can visit fine farmhouses and mills that my forebears built and owned centuries ago. I inherited know-how and opportunity from generations of intact family systems, social privilege, and access to institutions of society.

Most Black people in the United States are only a few generations removed from ancestors whose enslavers considered them property, prevented them from receiving education, and subjected them to great abuse, including tearing families apart. One and a half centuries since the abolition of slavery is a short time for a whole sector of society to heal from such brutalization, especially when the intervening years have included the reversal of Reconstruction, the horrors of Jim

Crow, disenfranchisement, discriminatory policies and laws, and other forms of racism and injustice.

ANTIRACISM MUST MOVE BEYOND GUILT TO ACTION

Being frozen with guilt for my privilege as a White male is unlikely to decrease racial polarization; I must move forward and act for justice. I can start by learning something of how the world looks from the perspective of Black people and other minorities. Today there are many resources to learn about the Black experience in America without expecting a minority person to once again repeat information readily available elsewhere.

Pastor Osheta Moore's book *Dear White Peacemakers* opened my eyes. While enfolding her White audience in an unexpected and unmerited blanket of love, this Black Anabaptist woman takes readers into harsh realities of racism and White supremacy. With a mix of storytelling, humor, and anger she explains the dehumanization that Black people routinely face. Even her attention to capitalization in writing has implications I had not considered. Unlike many writers, she capitalizes the word *White* when using it to identify people:

> I do this for two reasons: my capitalizing White as I write this book reminds me of your intrinsic worth to God. You are a human being. You are Beloved. . . . I capitalize to remind me to honor you in the same way I hope you'll honor me as a Black person. I also capitalize because I ascribe to the idea that capitalizing Black but not White is another form of normalizing Whiteness. When White is the standard, then there's really no need to denote it. White is not the standard. . . . Made in the image of God is the standard.[9]

Moore cautions White Christians against quickly citing Galatians 3:28 ("There is no longer Jew or Greek . . .") to deflect hard conversations about race. "The reality I live with in this Brown body," she states, "is that no matter how unified in Spirit I feel to my White brothers and sisters, at the end of the day, we live in a world deeply beholden to white supremacist ideas, systems, beliefs, policies, and postures that create comfort for them and struggle for me. Nothing about that feels reconciliatory."[10]

Moore writes about how *white* supremacy tore enslaved people from their native African cultures to the point that she has no idea what tribe her ancestors came from. The injustices continued. At the time of the Civil War, the US government briefly promised formerly enslaved people "forty acres and a mule." Tens of thousands received land, but President Lincoln's successor Andrew Johnson rescinded that allotment later that same year, 1865.[11] The Homestead Act of 1862 had given vast tracts of land taken from Indigenous people to White people, though some recipients were Black.[12] Many of them migrated to avoid oppression in the South. After the war, vigilantism and violence continued. The injustice took many forms, including lynching, which has claimed the lives of more than three thousand Black people.[13]

Today, Black men disproportionately die in police custody and Black women disproportionately die in childbirth. There are many such statistics and stories that put the experience of Black Americans in stark contrast. Though as a child Moore was an avid reader who qualified for advanced placement, her school put her in a remedial English class. In another example, she describes being pulled over by police for no apparent reason. She says,

You, as a White person, must learn how to enter into the great, unrelenting pain of people of color that has been caused by white supremacy. In entering in when you don't have to, when you could choose to ignore, you are walking in the way of Jesus. Get acquainted with our grief, mourn with us, and build a bridge with your compassion.[14]

Though Moore supports political activism to address systemic racism, her focus in *Dear White Peacemakers* is on calling White persons to commit "small, intentional acts of humility" that show love to Black and Brown neighbors. "You can do this," she says. "You are not alone."[15]

RELATIONSHIPS ACROSS ECONOMIC AND SOCIAL LINES CAN TRANSFORM LIVES

Church and society need contributions from people of all races. We also need urban, rural, religious, nonreligious, professional, working class, immigrant, and native-born. Most of us have at least superficial contact with persons different from ourselves while shopping, traveling, or pursuing vocation. But such exposure to diversity does not usually lead to the sustained relationships that are important to the kingdom of God. Jesus recognized that it is human nature to socialize only with persons like ourselves. But "when you give a luncheon or a dinner," he told followers, "invite the poor, the crippled, the lame, and the blind" (Luke 14:12–13).

A recent analysis of seventy-two million Facebook users shows that Jesus was on to something: Youth from poor families who have friendships that cut across economic and social class lines are more likely to be economically secure in adulthood.[16] Past and present national sins of America mean that economic and social divisions often coincide with racial lines.

The Facebook study report concluded that "cross-class friendships—what the researchers called economic connectedness—had a stronger impact than school quality, family structure, job availability or a community's racial composition. The people you know, the study suggests, open up opportunities, and the growing class divide in the United States closes them off. . . . In places where poor people have more rich friends, outcomes are better."[17] The researchers observed, however, that simply bringing people into physical proximity through school busing or affirmative action housing is not enough for economic transformation to happen. People have to form relationships.

A notable factor in the growth of the early church was cross-fertilization between economic and social classes,[18] and Christians were aware of the need for reciprocal relationships between rich and poor. When Paul urged economically blessed believers at Corinth to help needy Christians in Jerusalem, he said it was "a question of a fair balance between your present [material] abundance and their need, so that their [spiritual] abundance may be for your need" (2 Corinthians 8:13–14). The book of James (2:5) asks, "Has not God chosen the poor in the world to be rich in faith and to be heirs of the kingdom that he has promised to those who love him?" It is not only the wealthy or privileged who have gifts to offer to church and society.

The Facebook study revealed that rich people have mostly rich friends, and poor people have mostly poor friends. In a time when CEOs earn 351 times as much as the average worker, many people recognize the need for more equal distribution of income.[19] But there is also urgent need for different sectors of society to share life experience on how to access educational or vocational opportunities. The church can be an ideal place for that to happen.

Chapter 10
REFLECT AND DISCUSS

1. When and how did you first become aware of racism in society, in the church, or in yourself?

2. What is the racial mix of incarcerated people in your part of the world? Do you know persons affected by the school-to-prison pipeline? What assistance does church or government provide to persons coming out of prison?

3. What do you know about the history of White supremacist activity in your community, province, or state? What about redlining or "sundown" laws (which required Black people to leave town before sunset)?

4. How have friends, family, or mentors helped open vocational doors for you? Have you seen or experienced that kind of mentoring between rich and poor? Whom could you mentor? Who might serve as a mentor for you?

5. What questions does this chapter raise for you?

11

WHAT DRAWS *the* GLOBAL CHURCH TOGETHER?

How much agreement does a family, church, or nation need to function well? Humans do not all think or act alike—how boring that would be! But we all have seen polarities destroy families, churches, and nations. Such splintering can do severe damage and leave generations of mistrust. Maintaining common ground becomes especially important in matters of faith and worship, which reach deep into the soul.

HUMANITY MUST WORK TOGETHER TO SURVIVE

Nuclear weapons, climate change, and pandemics demonstrate that people of the world need to collaborate to survive. Beyond addressing such threats to our existence, diverse cultures can also enrich each other in educational, cultural, and entrepreneurial ways. Global entities that address threats or opportunities include the United Nations, the International Student Organization, Médecins Sans Frontières/Doctors Without Borders, the World Health Organization, and many others.

Comparable organizations did not exist in the first century, but Jesus nevertheless gave his followers a global mandate: "Make disciples of all nations, . . . teaching them to obey everything that I have commanded you" (Matthew 28:19–20). His last words on the Mount of Olives were "You will be my witnesses in Jerusalem, in all Judea and Samaria, and to the ends of the earth" (Acts 1:8). Power for this would come from the Holy Spirit, Jesus said. His disciples would bridge all cultural and political chasms, loving even their enemies. Living out that vision should put Christians at the forefront of international cooperation.

JESUS CHRIST IS THE CHURCH'S ONE FOUNDATION

Citizenship in a global kingdom of God became tangible for me in 2018 when I joined several hundred other denominational leaders for a gathering in Geneva, Switzerland. Delegates came from Orthodox, Pentecostal, Presbyterian, Coptic, Anglican, Lutheran, Mennonite, and many other churches. When organ music flooded the chapel and we sang, "The church's one foundation is Jesus Christ, her Lord," my eyes filled with tears of gratitude.

"For us as Christians," Pope Francis told the assembled church leaders, "walking together is not a ploy to strengthen our own positions, but an act of obedience to the Lord and love for our world. Whenever we say, 'Our Father,' we feel an echo within us of our being sons and daughters, but also of our being brothers and sisters."[1]

Images of sixteenth-century Anabaptists—my spiritual forebears—being burned at the stake came to mind as I worshiped with believers from other Christian traditions. The Anabaptist movement, from which the Mennonite church emerged, began at a time of catastrophic religious polarization in Europe. Christians were slaughtering each other, and some Anabaptists took up arms or publicly railed against those with whom they disagreed.

MY ANABAPTIST HERITAGE HAS POLARIZED ROOTS

How can the global church find unity when we still carry wounds from such unhappy events centuries later? *Anabaptist* means "re-baptizer," a contemptuous label hurled at those whose understanding of the Bible meant they rejected the practice of infant baptism that was nearly universal in Europe. To many Europeans of that era, it seemed politically dangerous and theologically offensive for anyone to be (re)baptized upon confession of faith when they had already been baptized as infants. How could European society hold together if some people were allowed to make their own rules?

Widespread social and economic unrest in Europe fanned flames of conflict. In 1524–25, throughout German-speaking parts of western Europe, peasants revolted against nobles and clergy who controlled land and taxes. This rebellion was a violent effort to dismantle oppressive economic and political structures, and upper classes mercilessly put it down. Some Anabaptist clergy supported the rebellion, in which up to one hundred thousand peasants perished.

Martin Luther wrote a tract entitled *Against the Murderous, Thieving Hordes of Peasants*. He condemned religious leaders of the rebellion, who he believed served the devil with the "outward appearance of the Gospel." Luther's 1530 Augsburg Confession, which covers a wide range of topics and specifically condemns Anabaptists, is still in use today.

A few years after Luther wrote the Augsburg Confession, an armed Anabaptist cabal seized the city of Münster, Germany. They set up a communitarian economy, anointed a king, legalized polygamy, and executed dissenters. Armies of neighboring powers promptly snuffed out the rebellion and its hopes for the imminent return of Christ. Anabaptist groups that survived elsewhere in Europe and became Mennonite never endorsed the militant extremism of Münster, but the reputation of Anabaptism suffered long-term damage.

IT MATTERS HOW WE REMEMBER OUR PAST

What happens to Christian unity when Lutherans today recite the Augsburg Confession with its condemnation of Anabaptists—whose spiritual descendants include today's Mennonites? What happens when Mennonites pore over the *Martyrs Mirror* with its wrenching images of Anabaptists being tortured by church or state officials—whose spiritual descendants are today's Lutherans and Catholics?

With such questions in mind, in 2002 Lutherans and Mennonites began to explore the possibility of formal reconciliation. Theologians and historians of the two churches met to explore issues and events that separated the groups. They worshiped together, built trust, and found many points of agreement. They heard each other's stories, then together wrote a shared narrative of what happened in the sixteenth century. Nobody wanted to ignore painful history, and all wanted "right remembering" that could be redemptive.

At a global gathering of Mennonites in Paraguay in 2009, General Secretary Ishmael Noko of Lutheran World Federation announced that Lutherans at their next global assembly would formally apologize for harm done to Anabaptists. Lingering Lutheran condemnations against Anabaptists were "like the poison which a scorpion carries in its tail," Noko said. "We have not struck out with this poison for some time, but we still carry it with us in our system."[2]

General Secretary Larry Miller of Mennonite World Conference later responded to Lutherans:

> For you, the witness of the Augsburg Confession is foundational and authoritative, an essential shaper of your identity. For [Mennonites], the witness of the Anabaptist martyrs is a living and vital story, retold in our global community of churches to build group identity.
>
> How can you distance yourself from the condemnations and their consequences while still honoring your history and strengthening your identity? How can we distance ourselves from use of the martyr tradition which perpetuates a sense of victimization and marginalization . . . while still honoring our history and strengthening our identity?[3]

Lutherans have not removed negative references to Anabaptists from the Augsburg Confession, and Mennonites have not stopped reading the *Martyrs Mirror*. But how we use and interpret our sacred stories has changed. We have gained new insight on perspectives of our former ecclesial opponents. We recognize acrimony of the past as reason for repentance and know that the other is committed to being in fellowship.

DENOMINATIONAL VARIETY ENRICHES THE BODY OF CHRIST

Such interaction between denominational groups highlights diversity in the Christian church. Variety is not surprising, since the author of Hebrews reminds us that God "spoke to our ancestors in many and various ways" (Hebrews 1:1). Allegiance to the incarnate Son is the most universal characteristic of Christian churches, and "no one can lay any foundation other than the one that has been laid" (1 Corinthians 3:11).

But church history shows that God has built on that foundation in countless ways.

I'm grateful for the ancient liturgies of Orthodox believers, the social justice witness of Roman Catholics, and the spiritual gifts of Pentecostals. I admire how African Christians dance their offerings to the altar, how Anglican choirs hallow a cathedral, how Black pastors in the United States preach with call-and-response. I treasure the Mennonite heritage of peacemaking, service, and (in North America) four-part harmony.

Aspects of other denominational expressions make me uncomfortable. My understanding of New Testament evidence, for example, means I do not endorse baptism of infants. But I can appreciate that some churches baptize infants out of the conviction that salvation comes entirely as a gift. That's an important reminder to Mennonites, since our emphasis on discipleship might tempt us to imagine that we can earn salvation.

GLOBAL MENNONITES NEEDED TO RECONCILE IN THE AFTERMATH OF WAR

Geography and politics can separate Christians from each other, making unity a near impossibility. Mennonites in Europe, for example, found themselves on opposite sides of World War I. Canada and the United States, with their considerable Mennonite populations, went to war against Germany. Some Mennonites in both Europe and North America—willingly or unwillingly—became armed foes in the murderous conflagration.[4]

But after guns fell silent, German Mennonite pastor Christian Neff dreamed of convening fellow church people from across Europe and beyond to restore or establish relationships. Following the precedent of Protestant denominations, Neff helped orchestrate a "Mennonite World Conference" gathering. About one hundred participants met in Basel, Switzerland, in 1925.[5]

Five years earlier, a relief project had planted seeds of international Mennonite cooperation. In the chaos after the Bolshevik Revolution, thousands of people in Ukraine—including Mennonites—faced famine. Collaborating with European and Canadian churches, American Mennonites in 1920 formed a "central committee" to aid people of Russia. It would later become Mennonite Central Committee.

Neff's Mennonite "world" conference was largely a European event. But Mennonites now began to think globally about their identity and witness. "The whole world," declared a preacher at the 1925 assembly, "which has lost the way of righteousness and peace, is looking to us to see whether they can possibly find in a little Christ-centered denomination the solution for the great problems now confronting them."[6]

A Dutch preacher acknowledged that Mennonites were only part of "the one great river of Christian life" that has many streams. Mennonites had to decide whether to "obey God just as much as the State allows" or to "obey the State as far as God allows." The preacher said the church "has to choose between the cannon and the cross, between war and Christ."[7] Pervading discussion in 1925 was desire for Christ-centered spirituality. "It is not the name 'Mennonite' that shall unite us," asserted a Frenchman, "nor the fact that we practice believer's baptism. It is not outward things that will bring us unity, but the attitudes of our heart, our love for the crucified and risen Saviour."[8]

BASIC SHARED CONVICTIONS CREATE A CORE OF UNITY

Since 1925, Mennonites from up to fifty-eight nations have gathered periodically for an assembly. In the past generation, unity that Mennonites cherish has brought ongoing collaboration in the time between assemblies through standing committees and networks. These focus on mission, peacemaking, pastoral care, theology, education, and more.

At a 2003 assembly, the global body tasked theologians from several continents with drafting a document that eventually became "Shared Convictions of Global Anabaptists" (see sidebar on next page). Wanting to do theology "from the bottom up" rather than "from the top down," authors of that document mined thirty-four Anabaptist statements of faith from around the world for points of agreement. Churches on every continent then had several years to critique and ratify a draft of the shared convictions.

"We cannot force or manufacture unity," said current Mennonite World Conference general secretary César García. "It is a gift of the Spirit that we receive." He noted that for seventy-five years, Mennonites collaborated without any written faith statement. "Ephesians calls us to *keep* that unity [Ephesians 4:1–6]. If we use confessions or statements of faith to *define* unity, then we are in trouble."[9]

With that in mind, the shared convictions appropriately do not speak to pastoral matters that lack widespread agreement. National Anabaptist and Mennonite churches, in their own contexts, still need to decide numerous practical things such as the status of LGBTQ people or the roles of women and men in leadership.

García is a native of Colombia, which has seen decades of war, and he noted the unifying effect of suffering on the body of Christ. "When you are in peace and prosperity," he said, "you have time to discuss issues that separate Christians, and to be critical. But when persecution or natural disaster threaten your life, you have to rely on each other. If there is an army outside the house looking for you, you are going to pray with other Christians regardless of their specific doctrinal or ethical beliefs."

SHARED CONVICTIONS OF GLOBAL ANABAPTISTS

By the grace of God, we seek to live and proclaim the good news of reconciliation in Jesus Christ. As part of the one body of Christ at all times and places, we hold the following to be central to our belief and practice:

1. God is known to us as Father, Son and Holy Spirit, the Creator who seeks to restore fallen humanity by calling a people to be faithful in fellowship, worship, service and witness.

2. Jesus is the Son of God. Through his life and teachings, his cross and resurrection, he showed us how to be faithful disciples, redeemed the world, and offers eternal life.

3. As a church, we are a community of those whom God's Spirit calls to turn from sin, acknowledge Jesus Christ as Lord, receive baptism upon confession of faith, and follow Christ in life.

4. As a faith community, we accept the Bible as our authority for faith and life, interpreting it together under Holy Spirit guidance, in the light of Jesus Christ to discern God's will for our obedience.

5. The Spirit of Jesus empowers us to trust God in all areas of life so we become peacemakers who renounce violence, love our enemies, seek justice, and share our possessions with those in need.

6. We gather regularly to worship, to celebrate the Lord's Supper, and to hear the Word of God in a spirit of mutual accountability.

7. As a world-wide community of faith and life we transcend boundaries of nationality, race, class, gender, and language. We seek to live in the world without conforming to the powers of evil, witnessing to God's grace by serving others, caring for creation, and inviting all people to know Jesus Christ as Saviour and Lord.

In these convictions we draw inspiration from Anabaptist forebears of the 16th century, who modelled radical discipleship to Jesus Christ. We seek to walk in his name by the power of the Holy Spirit, as we confidently await Christ's return and the final fulfillment of God's kingdom.

Adopted by Mennonite World Conference General Council, 2006

CAN WE HAVE UNITY AND STILL DISAGREE?

With the shared convictions reflecting the unity that Mennonites experience, would it be wise or possible to *discuss* matters on which we differ? At a Mennonite World Conference gathering of one hundred delegates in Kenya in 2018, a subcommittee brought a proposal called "Responding to Controversial Issues." The document proposed that if a member church wanted to address a controversial matter that went beyond the shared convictions, Mennonite World Conference leaders could authorize a formal process for discernment.

The proposed process would include Bible study, teaching sessions, and prayer. Participation would be optional, and diverse points of view would be welcome. The process would not necessarily legislate an outcome. The intention would be to shed light and gain wisdom rather than persuade or mandate. Could we trust each other that far?

Educator and author Stephen Covey says *trust* is the most essential element for organizations to remain healthy.[10] When changes happen or conflict arises, leaders must not move faster or further than the group is ready to trust. That helps explain what happened when Mennonite delegates discussed the controversial issues proposal.

Some delegates feared a hidden agenda. "This is about homosexuality," one person said immediately, not trusting the intent of the proposal. "We need to be careful of what we affirm and where we want to go." Some delegates feared that merely processing controversial issues without coming to a decisive conclusion would foment division. What if one part of the global church insisted on discussing matters that other regions did not want to address? Churches that chose not to participate might feel isolated.

Delegates from North America were generally more positive about the controversial issues proposal than those from the Global South. "It is the vocation of the church through the Holy Spirit to discern the mind and the will of God," said one North American. A European added that it is good "to have a procedure without excluding," but then seemed to have second thoughts: "Why do we have to discuss topics that are controversial? We have 'Shared Convictions.'" In other words, *let's not wade into deep waters of conflict if we already have our feet on firm ground of agreement.*

In the end, Mennonite delegates sent the controversial issues proposal back to committee for further work. I admit to some disappointment. My cultural background generally makes me welcome opportunities to consider different points of view. I would love to hear sisters and brothers from around the world share cultural, biblical, and pastoral perspectives on abortion, participation in government, nonviolent direct action, gender identity, and other topics.

But background and life experiences that shaped my instincts for dealing with hot topics will be different from those of sisters and brothers in other parts of the world. I respect persons who expressed caution and rejoice that delegates gathered in Kenya recognized the importance of safeguarding the unity Mennonites have already achieved.

GRASSROOTS COOPERATION STRENGTHENS RELATIONS IN THE BODY OF CHRIST

As we have seen, even within one denominational stream there can be wide differences of conviction. What popular culture in North America calls "Mennonite" can vary from horse-and-buggy Amish to liberal Mennonites at elite universities. We do not always show appreciation for each other. Mennonite theologian Tom Yoder Neufeld, who long has pressed for unity in the national and global church, observes that "divisions between world communions often are not as vexing as those within the subfamilies that make up a particular denominational stream." In fact, he says, "divisions grow more vexing the closer one gets to dynamics *within* denominations and especially within congregations."[11]

But diverse Mennonites have discovered that, at least in practical projects of relief and service, we can collaborate. Allegra Friesen Epp of Manitoba testifies to that. She recently completed an internship with Mennonite Church Canada's Indigenous-Settler Relations program and has volunteered with Community Peacemaker Teams in Canada, Colombia, and Palestine. Some people associate that kind of activism with the radical left, so I asked how she relates to conservative Christians. Friesen Epp talked about two stints of service she did with Mennonite Disaster Service, a domestic relief program which helps clean up and rebuild after floods or other catastrophes in Canada and the United States.

"When I worked alongside conservative volunteers," she recalled, "we had conversations about how to read the Bible, homosexuality, and women in ministry. Some people just shut me down, but others asked questions. Another young adult asked why I used the term 'Mother God' in our group prayer, and we talked for hours. I didn't change his mind, but I understood where he was coming from. That built friendship and trust."[12]

Friesen Epp learned that her conversation partner had recently lost a parent, and that gave opportunity to show compassion. "There's empathy when another person trusts you," she said. "When people have theology that excludes others, it can look judgmental. But when you get to know them, you might realize they are operating out of what they see as love. I have come to look for the best in people rather than the worst."

Friesen Epp continues to correspond with Old Order Mennonite women who were on assignment with her. "You treat people differently when they are your friends. You navigate the relationship with more care. You don't have to abandon your theological differences, but they don't take priority. You have a common cause, such as building a home for someone."

Much as she values relationships that develop when people work side by side, Friesen Epp wants more than polite collaboration. She longs for unity in her congregation and denomination but offered this caveat: "The church is less than helpful when we put so much emphasis on unity that we forget at what cost. Sometimes we think we are unified when we are just keeping people out."

Businessman Harold Friesen of Alberta also came to value collaboration in a common mission. Belonging to a theologically conservative church, Friesen told me that he grieves the acceptance of abortion in church and society. But he pointed to disaster relief projects as an example of how disagreeing Christians still can work together. "When you are physically engaged in a shared task," he observed, "similarities outweigh differences. But when relationships happen mostly through talking, it's much more theoretical. Doing something practical, you both have skin in the game; it's not just ideas."[13]

CHURCH UNITY IS ULTIMATELY A DIVINE GIFT

Simply swinging hammers side by side is not in itself fulfillment of Jesus' prayer in John 17 that the church be one, but it may be evidence that God is at work. Unity of the local, national, or global church is a divine gift, something we receive and live into rather than an outcome we engineer. The same Spirit that moves us to recognize our need for God can open our eyes to see our need for spiritual bonds with all who call Jesus Lord. Hebrews 2:10–12 reminds us that the Creator God is "bringing many children to glory," and "all have one Father." Jesus "is not ashamed to call them brothers and sisters," and neither should we hesitate to recognize our spiritual kin.

Chapter 11
REFLECT AND DISCUSS

1. What has been your experience of relating to people of other Christian denominations? How do those relationships differ from interaction with people of other world religions? What are the benefits or risks in such relationships?

2. Are there spiritual wounds, new or old, that still separate your congregation or denomination from other Christian groups? Has anyone tried to address those divisions from the past?

3. How should Christians celebrate strengths of their own denominational heritage without self-righteousness or judgmentalism? Did you inherit stereotypes of other Christian groups that may no longer be accurate or relevant (if they ever were)?

4. What spiritual practices or theological insights have you admired or learned from other denominations? What gifts does your own denominational tradition bring to the global church?

5. What structures or habits does your congregation or denomination have for processing controversial topics? Have you seen disputed issues being processed too slowly or too quickly? What happened?

6. What questions does this chapter raise for you?

12

DEEP SPIRITUAL WELLS CAN REPLENISH HOPE

Promoting body armor makes this pacifist uncomfortable, but the military imagery in Ephesians 6 is surprisingly relevant for ideological and spiritual confrontations of our day. As the apostle Paul says, we are in a struggle "not against enemies of blood and flesh, but against . . . cosmic powers of this present darkness" and "spiritual forces of evil" (6:12). Destructive forces in our world include disinformation, White supremacy, militant tribalism, idolatrous nationalism, and cult of authoritarian personality.

How do Christians confront such forces? The apostle Paul says we need the "whole armor of God." And what appropriate armor! We wear the "belt of truth," so urgently needed when many are wielding lies and half-truths. We don the "breastplate of righteousness [or justice]," and put on as shoes "whatever will make you ready to proclaim the gospel of peace." The shield of faith and helmet of salvation follow, and finally "the sword of the Spirit, which is the word of God" (6:13–17). We *speak* the word of God in the face of injustice and evil.

Such an outfit makes us unusual players in today's political and theological fray, especially if we engage the struggle with allegiance to the kingdom of God instead of to political party or social class. Our allegiance grows out of a *metanarrative*—an overarching story—that each of us carries, a story that helps us understand ourselves and our place in history.

THE WRONG METANARRATIVE CAN DISPLACE BAPTISM VOWS

Results can be disastrous when people adopt a malignant metanarrative, as events in Rwanda revealed a generation ago. In his book *Mirror to the Church*, Ugandan theologian Emmanuel Katongole reflects on the massacre that engulfed Rwanda in 1994 during that nation's civil war. In a country often described as the most Christian in Africa, Hutu and Tutsi people systematically slaughtered each other. Starting on Maundy Thursday of Holy Week, people across Rwanda took up machetes to butcher even fellow Christians with whom they long had fellowshipped. More than half a million died in three months, and even church buildings became killing chambers.

"What story is powerful enough to make people forget their baptisms in the very places where they happened?" Katongole asks.[1] Historically, the author asserts, differences between Hutus and Tutsis were minor. They spoke the same language, shared the same culture, intermarried, and had many levels of interaction.[2]

But Europeans who colonized Rwanda accentuated class differences between Hutus and Tutsis and hardened ethnic boundaries by requiring everyone to carry identity cards. Certain foreign missionaries decided that Tutsis were a superior "Semitic" people who deserved to lead society while Hutus belonged to a subservient race under the "curse of Ham" (see Genesis 9:20–27). This pushed a wedge between tribal groups, adding to pressures that finally exploded in a cataclysmic spasm of violence.

A BRIEF LITURGY ANCHORED ISRAELITE IDENTITY

What story, Katongole wondered, would be powerful enough to cause such lethal polarization? A metanarrative can do that, a story that groups use to explain and define where they came from, who they are, and where they are going. Ancient Israelites, for example, retold this metanarrative:

> A wandering Aramean was my ancestor; he went down into Egypt and lived there as an alien, few in number, and there he became a great nation, mighty and populous. When the Egyptians treated us harshly and afflicted us, by imposing hard labor on us, we cried to the LORD, the God of our ancestors; the LORD heard our voice and saw our affliction, our toil, and our oppression. The LORD brought us out of Egypt with a mighty hand and an outstretched arm, with a terrifying display of power, and with signs and wonders; and he brought us into this place and gave us this land, a land flowing with milk and honey. (Deuteronomy 26:5–10)

With this brief liturgy Israelites could explain their origin, their relationship with God, the reason they were in Canaan, and why they now were bringing an offering to Yahweh. The Israelite metanarrative was powerful enough to motivate their conquest of Jericho and the rest of Canaan. Other metanarratives attracted some Israelites, such as belief that the storm god Baal brought life, fertility, and salvation (1 Kings 18).

AMERICAN METANARRATIVES HAVE BEEN USED TO JUSTIFY CONQUEST

The American metanarrative has often included "city upon a hill" ideas about the role of the United States in the world.[3] European settlers used the concept of "manifest destiny" as a mandate to subdue the entire continent and perhaps other parts of the world.[4] White American metanarratives generally downplay the horrors of slavery and the genocide of Native peoples, highlighting instead the fact that the Declaration of Independence says "All men are created equal." Invoking such selective narratives, American political movements today sometimes claim they can restore the nation to an imagined era of mythical greatness.

American metanarratives commonly have a strong religious element: America once was or should become a Christian nation, and believers can "take America back for God."[5] Extreme versions of such metanarratives morph into theocratic tribalism that is hostile to immigrants, Zionist (giving unqualified support to the modern state of Israel), dismissive of climate change, and authoritarian.

Other American religious metanarratives feature heroes such as Rev. Dr. Martin Luther King Jr. and Dorothy Day. Advocates championing these metanarratives acknowledge the suffering of Black people, Indigenous peoples, and other marginalized groups. Salvation in this metanarrative often means pursuing systemic justice and racial equality rather than simply restoring personal relationship with God. Activists in this camp promote ethnic and gender inclusion.

Such contrasting political and theological stances can evolve into destructive tribalism. Entire sectors of church and society at either end of the spectrum become monolithic, with everyone in each sector claiming the same perspective on a wide range of issues. It is then a small step to despising fellow citizens or neighbors or even fellow church members ("those people") at another point on the continuum. When that happens, we become tribal, grounding our identity in a political movement or theological camp instead of in the kingdom of God.

A 2018 research report entitled *Hidden Tribes: A Study of America's Polarized Landscape* confirms that a substantial portion of Americans give blind allegiance to extremes on the left or the right. Much of this report is disheartening, but it also reveals something hopeful. Most political noise today comes from the third of Americans on the extreme "wings." That means two-thirds of Americans belong to what the authors call the "Exhausted Majority."[6] Persons in this large sector seem to be thinking for themselves rather than simply embracing a complete package of political or theological positions endorsed by a tribal group. People in this majority are more able to listen to another's point of view and more inclined to compromise.

Emmanuel Katongole says the Rwandan genocide should awaken Christians to the moral hazards of ideological tribalism. "Christian expression throughout the world has too easily allowed the blood of tribalism to flow deeper than the waters of baptism," he writes.[7] The commitment we make to Jesus Christ needs to take priority over all political, ethnic, or national allegiances even though this means the identity of Christians may seem "confused and confusing" to the world.[8] People will not be able to place us within familiar political or social tribes.

WE USE INADEQUATE OR INACCURATE LABELS

To what extent does tribalism infect American Christianity? Ordained minister Shana Peachey Boshart of Indiana agrees with Katongole that American Christians become partisan too easily. We start calling each other by labels intended to disparage, such as liberal or conservative. "Labeling makes it difficult to talk to each other," Boshart said. "A label brings preconceived notions that can be wrong. We act like people are in separate categories when most actually are somewhere on a continuum."[9]

In many churches, she adds, a person's openness to LGBTQ inclusion has become *the* litmus test of whether they are liberal or conservative. "But pick another topic and people might fall elsewhere on the continuum," she said. In her denomination, for example, there is a breadth of perspectives on whether the communion table should be open to all who wish to participate. "In the whole life of the church this and many other topics also matter," she said.

Two decades of church leadership have given Boshart wisdom for staying spiritually strong amid conflict and competing demands. The first spiritual resource she mentions is attention to scripture, which for her includes listening to the *Pray as You Go* and *Bible Project* podcasts. Being attentive to beauty in the world also nurtures her spirit, and corporate worship has been indispensable. "I don't always feel like going to church on Sunday morning," she allowed, "but God has chosen the church as the vehicle for transforming the world."

OUR METANARRATIVE IS GOD'S REDEMPTIVE ACTION IN THE WORLD

For all believers, regardless of where we find ourselves in a fractured ecclesial or political landscape, our task is to be agents of healing. Christians should treasure the Old Testament metanarrative, but our defining story is the life, death, and resurrection of Jesus. A few words can summarize the Christian metanarrative: "In Christ God was reconciling the world to himself, not counting their trespasses against them, and entrusting the message of reconciliation to us. So we are ambassadors for Christ, since God is making his appeal through us" (2 Corinthians 5:19–20).

Reconciliation begins with peace in our personal lives and peace within the church. Paul tells the Galatians that the whole of Jewish law can be summarized in a single commandment: "You shall love your neighbor as yourself." He exhorts readers not to "bite and devour one another," to avoid "enmities, strife, jealousy, anger, quarrels, dissensions, factions, envy." The hallmark of Christian community will be fruit of the Spirit: love, joy, peace, patience, kindness, generosity, faithfulness, gentleness, and self-control (Galatians 5:14–26).

In the book of Romans, Paul's great treatise on grace, the apostle addresses believers in the polarized hub of the empire. Tensions within the Jewish community at Rome, perhaps exacerbated by Christian proclamation, had become so alarming that Emperor Claudius a few years earlier had expelled the entire troublesome community (Acts 18:2).[10] When Paul wrote his epistle to Rome, Emperor Nero was on the throne, and Jews apparently had returned. But Nero would eventually slaughter Christians, and his reign ended with civil war.

The apostle gives pointed instructions on how followers of Jesus should conduct themselves amid conflicts within the church, the Jewish community, or pagan society:

> Do not be conformed to the world. . . . Let love be genuine; . . . love one another with mutual affection; outdo one another in showing honor. . . . Extend hospitality to strangers. . . . Live in harmony with one another . . . do not claim to be wiser than you are. . . . So far as it depends on you, live peaceably with all. . . . Overcome evil with good. (Romans 12:2, 9–10, 13, 16, 18, 21)

What a code of conduct for Christian testimony in a polarized society! Living that way requires deep spiritual wells.

EXTREME POLARIZATION CALLS FOR
RECONCILIATION MINISTRY

From the late 1960s until 1998, polarization and violence known as the Troubles plagued Northern Ireland. The roots of this conflict stretch back to the seventeenth century, when Protestant settlers from England and Scotland occupied "unplanted" (actually, confiscated) farmland in Ireland. Thus began centuries of tension between the native Catholic majority of Ireland who wanted independence and Protestant settlers who remained loyal to the British crown.

Opposing Protestant and Catholic paramilitaries (unofficial armed forces) emerged in Northern Ireland during the late twentieth century. Both sides used political propaganda, public marches, assassinations, and bombings to sway public opinion. More than thirty-five hundred people died, and some violence spilled over into England. When my family and I lived in London (1991 to 1996), the roar of an Irish Republican Army terrorist bomb jolted us two times.

Visionary Christian leaders in Northern Ireland—notably at Corrymeela community—worked valiantly to bridge this polarization. At Belfast, a Presbyterian layman named Joe Campbell spent decades fostering conversation across the sectarian divide. Educated as a high school teacher, Campbell served as a mentor for young people at risk of being caught up in the Troubles. "The pathway of school failure, unemployment, social deprivation, and political violence was well-worn in Northern Ireland," Campbell said. A graduate degree in conflict transformation from Eastern Mennonite University gave him tools to mediate in political, community, and congregational conflicts.[11]

FORMER ENEMIES MEET FACE-TO-FACE
IN NORTHERN IRELAND

I once had the opportunity to accompany Joe Campbell as he met secretly in Belfast with a dozen paramilitary men—six Protestants and six Catholics. All had served time in prison, and some had killed. Campbell and a colleague had established relationships with these individuals when they were behind bars. "Men in prison in a conflict such as this have a critical influence on what happens outside," Campbell explained, "and they have time on their hands to ponder and reflect."

To avoid suspicion, the unarmed men arrived one or two at a time at our meeting place. Campbell later described them as "insider partials." He meant that they remained fully committed to their sectarian cause but had developed the capacity to respect at least the *person* if not the *cause* on the other side. They were ready to talk, and their cordiality surprised me. *We don't want our sons to do what we have done* they all agreed.

That improbable meeting took place because Campbell and other visionaries worked below radar for years to build trust. Ever ready to credit others, Campbell said that Quakers and Mennonites who helped initiate such peacemaking work in Northern Ireland "punched above their weight." Not a usual pacifist metaphor, the phrase refers to a boxer taking on a larger opponent. The larger opponent in Northern Ireland was severe political and social polarization.

The Good Friday Agreement in Ireland (1998) that ended most violence of the Troubles grew out of a public political process and appropriately got international attention. Largely invisible was the quiet "track two" diplomacy of Joe Campbell and many others who helped prepare whole communities for an end to bloodshed.

SPIRITUAL DISCIPLINES SUSTAIN A PEACEMAKER

Not long after that meeting with paramilitaries, I asked Campbell how he could sustain such arduous and risky peacemaking ministry over a period of years. "You have to have deep spiritual wells," he said quietly. When I asked him recently what he had meant by that, he wrote,

> In a long-term conflict, it was always clear to me that I needed to pace myself. Conflict drains people, and in Ireland too many became exhausted, burned out, and never returned to the task.
>
> One deep well for me has been the practice of daily prayer, Bible reading, and meditation. I also have taken every opportunity for public worship in a variety of settings. These have been ways of keeping refreshed so that I have something to offer those that I walk alongside in conflict.
>
> Being part of a small group or network of friends who share life, pray together, and gently hold one another to account has been another deep well. Prayer has been central, because of how easy it is in violent settings, when friends and neighbors have been killed, to be overcome by despair, anger, and revenge.
>
> For several years I went to the location where a bomb had exploded or a person had been shot dead to stand quietly in prayer for the family and friends, asking God for healing and hope. In those times I needed the Spirit to remind me that God is sovereign over creation and over history. I asked that my heart would not be hardened but would remain malleable and ever open to see God even in dark and fearful times.[12]

In a ministry where visible change was often hard to discern, Campbell found it essential to have activities that took him away from the stress of conflict. He became an accomplished gardener and regularly skippered a small sailboat in Belfast Harbour. "My primary calling has always been to serve the Lord in peace work," Campbell said, "but these diversions have been aids to sustain me for the long haul."

CORPORATE WORSHIP PRACTICES CAN SUSTAIN MINISTRY AND BUILD UNITY

Eleanor Kreider agrees with Joe Campbell that preparation for reconciliation witness requires more than individual spiritual practices. For thirty years she taught mission and peacemaking in the British Isles, and now in retirement she ministers among congregations in North America. Concerned about toxic polarization in British and American societies, she sees the church as a primary channel of God's healing presence in the world. Theology of worship is her special interest. When I interviewed her, she sat at a table stacked with hymnbooks and prayer resources.

"I've just leafed through our church's hymnal," she said, "looking for hymns celebrating and calling for unity in the local congregation." She pointed to an old favorite, "We Are One in the Spirit," and also to the hymn "One Is the Body" by Scot John Bell, which speaks of the oneness of the church and its Head, the oneness of the Spirit "by whom we are led."[13] Most hymnbooks do not have an abundance of songs about congregational unity, but there are other ways to accent the theme in worship. "Every congregation can mine the poetry, dance, and visuals of artistically gifted members to help express this topic that is so rich in scripture," she said.[14]

When using the Lord's Prayer in public worship, Kreider suggests, the worship leader can highlight sibling ties among all believers: "Let us join together in one Spirit as we pray to *our Father.*" An invitation to communion can remind worshipers that Jesus, host of the eucharist table, washed his disciples' feet in humble service, loved his enemies, and prayed that his followers "may be one."

Baptism can explicitly celebrate unity of the church. "In the waters of baptism," Kreider continued, "we commit ourselves not only to God, but to one another in accountability." The apostle Paul names the polarities of Jew and Greek, enslaved and free, then rejoices that "in the one Spirit we were all baptized into one body . . . and we were all made to drink of one Spirit" (1 Corinthians 12:13). This unity is a gift, brought by Christ who created "one new humanity" through the cross (Ephesians 2:15).

Jesus' unity prayer in John 17 is passionate, Kreider observed. "With his imminent departure, he sensed that danger lurked. He prayed, 'Holy Father, while I was with them, I protected them . . . and not one of them was lost. . . . Protect them from the evil one.'" On Jesus' mind was the ever-present risk of dissension stirred up by the evil one.

"We can light a peace candle as a call for unity within the body of Christ, not only for peace between nations," Kreider suggested. Closely related is "passing the peace," one of the most ancient expressions of Christian fellowship. "This can be more than just saying 'Hi, nice to see you.'" A worship leader can preface passing the peace with scripture and words that acknowledge the gift of oneness among diverse members. "This can renew our commitment to worship and work together. Public prayers can include petition for unity of the church locally and globally."

THE SPIRIT GIVES UNITY FOR RECONCILING MISSION IN THE WORLD

On the night before he died, Jesus gave his followers a "new commandment" that they love one another: "By this everyone will know that you are my disciples, if you have love for one another" (John 13:34–35). Unity within the body of Christ is not optional or aspirational; it is a gift of God and an essential part of obedience to our Lord for effective witness in the world.

When Jesus appeared to his disciples on Resurrection Sunday, he prepared them for mission. Fear had isolated followers of Jesus behind locked doors. "Peace be with you," declared the risen Lord (John 20:19–21). Then he showed wounds in his hands and side that came from daring to reach across chasms of spiritual and political polarization. "Peace be with you," he repeated. "As the Father has sent me, so I send you."

Chapter 12
REFLECT AND DISCUSS
1. Can you give examples of what it might mean in a polarized world for you to "wear the belt of truth," the "breastplate of righteousness/justice," and the "shoes of peace"? What actions or practices might this "body armor" entail?

2. Have you seen or experienced what it looks like when Christians "allow the blood of tribalism to flow deeper than the waters of baptism"? What tug of political, social, or ethnic identity might tend to pull you more than your commitment to Jesus?

3. When have you experienced Bible study, prayer, song, or corporate worship shaping you in the way of Jesus? How often are you aware of that kind of spiritual formation? What diversions or hobbies help sustain you for peacemaking or other aspects of witness?

4. What aspects of this book give you hope about polarization in church or society? What remaining questions, concerns, or ideas do you have?

CONCLUSION

I write these closing words from Jerusalem, one of the most polarized places on earth. Jews, Muslims, and Christians sometimes have collaborated well here over the centuries. But tension between adherents of these great religions has often spawned violence. Today, an ominous wall snakes through East Jerusalem and on for four hundred miles, stark symbol of unhappy polarization between Israeli and Palestinian. Bethlehem, where hope came into the world, is on the other side of the wall from where I sit.

Jesus once looked over Jerusalem from the Mount of Olives and said, "If you . . . had only recognized on this day the things that make for peace!" (Luke 19:42). He taught his followers what makes for peace, but we don't always show it. The six Christian communions who share administration of the Church of the Holy Sepulcher in Jerusalem have had trouble getting along for centuries. In an 1846 clash between Latin and Greek Christians, "rival groups of worshippers fought not only with their fists, but with crucifixes, candlesticks, chalices, lamps and incense-burners, and even bits of wood which they tore from the sacred shrines."[1] More than forty people lay dead on the floor.

Christians in North America are not killing each other in sectarian violence today, thank God, and few people in our polarized society have resorted to physical violence. But at least figuratively, Christians sometimes clobber one another with crucifixes, and ideologues in wider society assault opponents with placards, websites, lawsuits, and sneers.

VENTURING BEYOND THE FAULT LINES

This book has traced a variety of fault lines in church and society—from the way faith communities use the Bible in relating to LGBTQ members to the experience of Indigenous and Black peoples in American history. At the beginning we highlighted how small actions can have enduring consequences and encouraged readers to take even seemingly insignificant steps toward healing in a polarized world. (See appendix A, "Options for Action," for a starting list.) Taking such steps may not change the world, but they change us.

Drawing from the work of Jonathan Haidt, we considered how differing moral foundations can lead people to contrasting points of view. This insight might give us understanding—even empathy—for persons with whom we disagree. Contrasting attitudes in Ezra and Ruth toward outsiders serve as an example of polarities in the Bible.

Rather than viewing biblical polarities as a problem, we might find them to be a valuable resource. They can remind us that the Spirit of God has moved in diverse ways among faith communities over the centuries. God does not change, but the context of divine initiative changes. We are right to have firm convictions in faith and practice, but perhaps we can relax a bit about relating to others who disagree with us; perhaps we can be willing to learn. Even sharp contrasts of conviction in a church or a nation can be healthy if adherents respect each other and still celebrate what they have in common.

We saw that Jesus lived in a society more polarized than ours yet established relationships with persons of astonishingly diverse politics and theology. He was no chameleon, changing colors to suit every situation. Nor did he retreat into an echo chamber where all voices said the same thing. Rather, he engaged the whole spectrum of belief in Jewish society with consistent love and authority. This is how Jesus wants his disciples to function, though it may be costly to risk such relationship-building. Take up your cross daily, he told followers (Luke 9:23). Little room for naïve optimism in that call.

Writings of the apostle Paul have been the theological and ecclesial backdrop for much of our study. Paul was a visionary who applied Jesus' teaching to the life of the church. As an ambassador who took the gospel to the ends of the earth, Paul ultimately laid down his life bridging the polarity between Jew and Gentile. His confidence that God will someday unite all things in Christ gave him hope to carry the gospel even to the capital of the Roman Empire that had killed his Lord.

The apostle Paul's passion to reach beyond boundaries of the faith community opened the way for our consideration of modern ambassadors of reconciliation—from Peace Chief Lawrence Hart in Oklahoma to Angela Tanner in inner-city Elkhart, Indiana. Joe Campbell of polarized Belfast showed us that sustained peacebuilding requires deep spiritual wells—prayer, faith community, Bible study, and rest.

WE MOVE THROUGH BROKENNESS AND SUFFERING TO HOPE AT THE EMPTY TOMB

This book presents no grand human strategy to save the church or the world from destructive polarization. Salvation belongs to God, and that is all we need to know to align with God's self-revelation in Jesus Christ. Because the kingdom of God that Jesus proclaimed is already breaking into history, Christians live now by its standards. We wash feet, forgive others, and love enemies. We do not seek suffering or romanticize martyrdom but make our lives a living sacrifice to God who "so loved the world." In the church we experience a foretaste of the New Jerusalem, the community of reconciliation with the Lamb at the center.

That foretaste is always partial, and we cannot expect the church to be perfect. On a ledge above the main entrance to the Church of the Holy Sepulcher, a small ladder has leaned against the façade since at least 1728. No one remembers exactly who put it there or why. But the six Christian denominations who administer the church know they must achieve unanimous consent before making *any* physical changes in the building. For almost three centuries they have been unable to agree on removing a worthless ladder. Perhaps the ladder is a symbol of mutual accountability between denominations, but I find the brokenness of the body of Christ painful.

My own brokenness compels me to go under the old ladder and through the church door to Calvary immediately inside. An Anabaptist like me may be put off by the encrusted layers of pious ornament heaped upon the rock where, by tradition, the cross of Jesus stood. But this is where God's love for a polarized and sinful world went the furthest. Here God incarnate paid with his life for standing up to destructive forces of alienation. Here Jesus suffered for my sin. I realize at Calvary that my own soul becomes polarized between who God made me to be and who I actually am.

From Calvary I continue inside the great church to the empty tomb, also heavily laden with icon and symbol. Alas, the entire structure of the tomb where Joseph of Arimathea buried Jesus was quarried away in early centuries of the Christian era. All that remains is the burial slab on which the body of Jesus lay, and that slab lies within a house-like shrine called the Edicule. Only once have I stood in the long line of pilgrims waiting to enter the holy site.

I need not pause long at the Edicule, since "he is not here; he has risen" (Matthew 28:6 NIV). In history's supreme act of vindication, God raised Jesus from the dead after powers of sin had done their worst. Now, along with Paul I say, "I want to know Christ and the power of his resurrection" (Philippians 3:10). That power is hope for healing of my own soul and healing of a polarized world. Am I ready to be an ambassador of that healing, even if the cost is high? In verse 10, Paul says that knowing the power of Christ's resurrection includes "the sharing of his sufferings by becoming like him in his death." Am I that committed to restoration of wholeness in church and society?

The Church of the Holy Sepulcher symbolizes most of what we need to know about God's response to destructive polarization—from the ladder of division to the cross where Jesus confronted the powers to the empty tomb where God began to restore all things. But somewhere nearby, exact location unknown, God supercharged the early Christian movement. Wind and fire of the Holy Spirit came upon followers of Jesus, and they began to speak about God's power to Jews "from every nation under heaven" living in Jerusalem (see Acts 2:5–13).

This was no *reversal* of the Tower of Babel fiasco, when God scrambled human languages (Genesis 11:1–9). Instead of having humans revert to a single language at Pentecost, the Holy Spirit enabled believers to translate the gospel into many cultures and languages. Onlookers from at least sixteen regions of the ancient world heard the gospel in their own tongue, a harbinger of the rich diversity of Christian expression that would follow.

Three thousand believed in Jesus at Pentecost and carried hope in all directions. They left Jerusalem just like you and I go into the world—one step at a time. Small steps, big steps, always toward God's future of wholeness in diversity, always linked to fellow ambassadors, always announcing good news. I want to be part of a redeemed people taking up such ministry to a fractured world, participating in God's plan to make "one new humanity" in Jesus Christ.

Maranatha! Come, Lord Jesus!

Appendix A

OPTIONS *for* ACTION

Rather than proposing large-scale remedies for polarization in church and society, this book focuses on understanding our differences and considering modest steps that individuals or groups can take. Below are a few options for action that might seem small, but doing them can have a cumulative effect that shapes our reflexes and sustains witness.

- Practice daily disciplines of prayer, Bible reading, and meditation with particular attention to themes of reconciliation.
- Memorize Isaiah 2:2–4, selections of Matthew 5–7, or other reflex-shaping Bible passages.
- Pray the Lord's Prayer daily, paying particular attention to "as we forgive . . ."
- Put a mezuzah on your doorpost as a daily reminder of allegiance to God alone.
- Share meals with other peacemaking Christians to relate stories, build solidarity, and plan reconciling witness.
- Learn and tell stories of reconciliation, celebrating heroes who bridged polarities.
- Surprise someone alienated from you with an act of generosity.

- Ask a neighbor whose politics you do not like to do some kindness for you, then respond with kindness of your own.
- Spend less time on social media and more time building face-to-face relationships, including with people outside your comfort zone.
- Explore your ancestry to learn about your racial/ethnic background.
- Learn about Japanese internment camps in the United States and Canada during World War II.
- Learn to know Indigenous people in your area. Visit museums of Indigenous art and history.
- Research the original and present-day Indigenous inhabitants of the land where you live; contribute to Indigenous groups or organizations, such as by naming them in your will.
- Form or join a group of politically or theologically diverse people who meet to build relationships.
- Participate in a Colossian Forum or Braver Angels workshop or conversation.
- Initiate respectful "track two" conversation with someone whose political or theological stance you do not understand or accept; listen well.
- Learn a language spoken by new immigrants to your community or find other ways to connect with these new neighbors.
- Learn more about the history and experience of Black people in America by reading *Dear White Peacemakers* or similar books.
- Incorporate commitment to church unity in public worship, including baptism and communion.

- Balance your work for peace with enough recreation to remain emotionally healthy.
- Use *Stuck Together* as a study guide for discussion in a small group or adult education class.

Appendix B

IT MATTERS WHERE WE GET OUR NEWS *and* COMMENTARY

There is no going back to the days when a few respected television networks or newspaper franchises kept us informed on current events. The internet genie is out of the bottle, and we now have an abundance of information sources. Websites and social media feature a wide range of responses to events in the world. Some are accurate, with facts supported by empirical data. Others distort with prejudice, highly selective reporting, or outright lies. Some sources of information polarize by design; others build communication and mutual respect.

Though all news and opinion sources present facts, it is important to know whether these are part of broadly documented reporting or just select anecdotes. Along with accuracy, Christians might look for the following values in news reports, commentary, or political messages:

1. *Is there concern for global, not just national or local, interests?* Christians properly give allegiance to the global kingdom of God rather than to only one country.

2. *Is there a preference for nonviolent ways of solving
    conflict?* Jesus' example would teach us not to glorify
    military or coercive solutions.
3. *Is there respect for people of other cultures and reli-
    gions?* Sneering, prejudice, and fearmongering harm
    the world that "God so loved" (John 3:16).
4. *Is there compassion for those who suffer at the
    margins?* Jesus and the Hebrew prophets taught us
    to care for immigrants, victims of bigotry, and other
    vulnerable people.
5. *Is there concern for care of the natural world?*
    Respecting God's creation means we will seek remedy
    for global warming, loss of species, and depletion of
    the earth's resources.
6. *Is there commitment to preserve human life?* All
    people should have adequate healthcare, education,
    and employment. Jesus would not support warfare
    or capital punishment, and would always seek to
    preserve life.

No news source, politician, or historian will match all the
values of Jesus or the Hebrew prophets. But some information sources leave more room than others for Sermon on the
Mount priorities. Some "Christian" news sources or political
voices reflect values antithetical to the way of Jesus. Since I
want to learn from a variety of perspectives and sources, I try
to scan several reputable national or international newspapers
and access both liberal and conservative media.

Appendix C

POSSIBILITIES *for* FURTHER READING

Izzeldin Abuelaish, *I Shall Not Hate: A Gaza Doctor's Journey on the Road to Peace and Human Dignity* (New York: Bloomsbury, 2011).

David Blankenhorn, *In Search of Braver Angels: Getting Along Together in Troubled Times* (New York: Braver Angels, 2022).

Peter T. Coleman, *The Way Out: How to Overcome Toxic Polarization* (New York: Columbia University Press, 2021).

Stephen M. R. Covey, *The Speed of Trust: The One Thing That Changes Everything* (New York: Free Press, 2006).

James Calvin Davis, *Forbearance: A Theological Ethic for a Disagreeable Church* (Grand Rapids, MI: Eerdmans, 2017).

Roxanne Dunbar-Ortiz, *An Indigenous Peoples' History of the United States* (Boston: Beacon Press, 2014).

Elaine Enns and Ched Meyer, *Healing Haunted Histories: A Settler Discipleship of Decolonization* (Eugene, OR: Cascade, 2021).

David E. Fitch, *The Church of Us vs. Them: Freedom from a Faith That Feeds on Making Enemies* (Grand Rapids, MI: Brazos, 2019).

Melissa Florer-Bixler, *How to Have an Enemy: Righteous Anger and the Work of Peace* (Harrisonburg, VA: Herald Press, 2021).

Jonathan Haidt, *The Righteous Mind: Why Good People Are Divided by Politics and Religion* (New York: Vintage, 2012).

Katherine Hayhoe, *Saving Us: A Climate Scientist's Case for Hope and Healing in a Divided World* (New York: One Signal, 2021).

Emmanuel M. Katongole, *Mirror to the Church: Resurrecting Faith after Genocide in Rwanda* (Grand Rapids, MI: Zondervan, 2009).

Matthew D. Kim and Paul A. Hoffman, *Preaching to a Divided Nation: A Seven-Step Model for Promoting Reconciliation and Unity* (Grand Rapids, MI: Baker Academic, 2022).

Ezra Klein, *Why We're Polarized* (New York: Avid Reader, 2020).

John Paul Lederach, *Reconcile: Conflict Transformation for Ordinary Christians* (Harrisonburg, VA: Herald Press, 2014).

Osheta Moore, *Dear White Peacemakers: Dismantling Racism with Grit and Grace* (Harrisonburg, VA: Herald Press, 2021).

Roy M. Oswald, *Managing Polarities in Congregations: Eight Keys for Thriving Faith Communities* (Herndon, VA: Alban Institute, 2010).

Kirsten Powers, *Saving Grace: Speak Your Truth, Stay Centered, and Learn to Coexist with People Who Drive You Nuts* (New York: Convergent, 2021).

David W. Shenk, *A Gentle Boldness: Sharing the Peace of Jesus in a Multi-Faith World* (Harrisonburg, VA: Herald Press, 2021).

INDEX

The letter *t* following a page number denotes a table.

abortion, 19–20, 36, 40, 43, 57, 133, 189, 191
Achtemeier, Paul, 146
African Americans: genetics, 234n8; and trauma, 90–91
Alexander the Great, 57
American Philosophical Society, 74–75
Amish, 30–31, 160, 189, 228n4 (ch. 1)
Anabaptists, 180–87
Arbery, Ahmaud Marquez, 230n4
Aryan Nation, 168–69
Augsburg Confession, 181–83

Babel, Tower of, 213
Babylonian exile, 44, 56, 71
ban (*herem*), 48
baptism: believers, 181, 184–185, 187; of infants, 181, 184; of Jesus, 68; of Saul, 139; as sign of unity, 196, 199, 206, 208, 216; vows, 196
Barmen, Theological Declaration of, 79
Bell, John, 205
Bible: diversity in, 20, 22, 24, 40–41, 83–84, 79–80; formation of, 39, 45; God-breathed, 124–25
Bible Project, 200
Black Kettle, 156–538
Black Lives Matter, 170–71
Blankenhorn, David, 115–16
Boshart, Shana Peachey, 199–200
boundaries, 14, 39–53, 62, 80, 85, 107–108, 138, 211

Braiding Sweetgrass, 152
Braver Angels, 114–16, 216
Bury My Heart at Wounded Knee, 152

Caesar Augustus, 137
Caiaphas, 230n1
Campbell, Joe, 202–205
Carlisle (PA) Indian Industrial School, 150
Carter, Jesse, 172–173
CEO salaries, 177
Cheyenne: cultural center, 154. *See also* Hart, Lawrence; Washita massacre
Christian Pledge of Allegiance, 229n4 (ch. 4)
church: boundaries of, 43–44; divisions in, 121; factions in, 60–63
citizenship, 82, 180
Civil War (American), 55–56, 175
Claudius (emperor), 201, 237n10
Clear, James, 32
climate change, 61, 153
Coleman, Peter, 21
collection for Jerusalem, 141–42
Colossian Forum, 113–14, 216
Colossians, 113
communion, 200, 206, 216
Community Peacemaker Teams, 190
conflict transformation, 103–104
Constantine (emperor), 96
Corinth, 77, 82–84, 108, 112, 130–31, 143, 177
Corrymeela community, 202
Covey, Stephen, 188

COVID-19, 17–18
critical race theory (CRT), 151–52
Curtiss, Victoria G., 112
Custer, Lt. Col. George Armstrong, 156–58

Day, Dorothy, 198
Dead Sea Scrolls, 59
Dear White Peacemakers, 174–76, 216
dentist's office (COVID-19 story), 17–18
Deuteronomy: annihilate Canaanites, 48;
    eunuchs and foreigners, 47; foreigners
    not admitted, 47; "Hear, O Israel," 31;
    remember you were a slave, 158–59;
    wandering Aramean, 197
discernment processes, 106–112, 121,
    125–131, 231n4
diversity: of God's people, 22–23, 48,
    183–84, 214; not adequate alone, 111–12;
    racial, 94; in relationships, 176; in
    scripture, 204, 40, 69, 76–79, 83–84
Durant, Will, 95

Eastern Mennonite University, 202
Ehrman, Bart, 228n3
Elijah (prophet), 110
Elkhart (IN) Police Department, 169
emperor worship, 58, 77–78, 137
Ephesians: gather up all things in Christ, 21;
    resurrection, 22; unity, 186; whole armor
    of God, 195
Epp, Allegra Friesen, 190
Essenes, 59, 68
Ethiopian eunuch, 138
ethnoi, 233n9 (ch. 8)
Eusebius, 233n8 (ch. 8)
evangelism, 62, 91
Ezekiel (book of), 50
Ezra (scribe/priest), 41–44

Facebook study on friendship, 176–77
Fair Housing Act (1968), 172–73
1 Corinthians, 23–24, 183
1 Peter, 23
Fitch, David, 113
flag (American), 77, 90–91, 101
Floyd, George, 170, 172
food offered to idols, 77, 79, 143–44
Francis I (pope), 149, 180
Franklin, Benjamin, 74–75
Friesen, Harold, 191
Funk, John, 159

Galatians, 110, 175, 201
Gamaliel, 52

García, César, 186
gas thieves story, 27–29, 37
genocide, 48, 162, 198–99
Gentiles, 67, 105, 110, 124–30
Gethsemane, 69
Great Migration, 172
"great replacement" conspiracy theory,
    93–94
Guatemala, 135–36
Gulker, Michael, 113–14
gun control, 167

Haidt, Jonathan, 33–35, 210
Hart, Betty, 150, 155
Hart, Lawrence, 150, 153–57
Hebrews (book of), 183
Helena (queen of Adiabene), 141
henotheism, 228n3
Hermas, Shepherd of, 235n18
Herodians, 58, 60, 63–64
Herod the Great, 58, 60, 137
Hillel (rabbi), 50–52
Holy Spirit, 82, 112, 126–27, 129–130, 180,
    187t, 189, 213
Homestead Act (1862), 175

idols, food offered to, 77, 79, 143–44
immigrants, 36, 92–93, 149, 159, 198, 216,
    235n13
Immigration and Customs Enforcement
    (ICE), 75
Indigenous peoples: conciliation with, 163;
    culture and history, 149–55, 175; geno-
    cide of, 79, 149, 155, 161; reparations to,
    160–63. See also *individual people groups*
*Indigenous People's History of the United
    States, An*, 152
Indigenous-Settler Relations program, 190
Indigenous territories, map of, 234n13
Ireland, Northern, 202–205
Isaiah (book of): inclusive welcome, 47, 49;
    mountain of the Lord, 30, 49; reason
    together, 169

James, 128–129; book of, 169, 177
Jeremiah (prophet), 25, 73–74, 110
Jerusalem: Church of the Holy Sepulcher,
    209–213; Jewish believers at, 126;
    Romans destroyed, 80; wall in modern
    city, 209
Jerusalem Council (Acts 15), 67, 127–29
Jeschke, Marlin, 230n12
Jesus Christ: authorities wanted to kill,
    89; broke down walls, 132; entry into

Jerusalem, 138; foundation of church, 84; model for relationships, 22, 25, 69; resurrection appearance, 207; unity prayer, 121–22, 191, 206

Jewish revolt, 56, 68–69, 137, 233n8 (ch. 8)

Jim Crow laws, 151–52, 173–74

John (Gospel of): Jesus' action in temple, 65; mission, 207; Nicodemus, 88–89; unity prayer, 206; woman taken in adultery, 84

John of Patmos, 78–81

John the Baptist, 64, 68

Johnson, Andrew (US president), 175

Johnson, Luke Timothy, 232n5

Johnson, Maj. Gen. Kermit D., 95–100

Jonah (prophet), 44–45, 48–49

Josephus, 137, 141

Judas, 84

Kansa (Kaw) people, 159–61

Katongole, Emmanuel, 196–99

Kauffman, Richard, 109

Kaur, Valerie, 99–100

Keller, Sheryl, 37

Kimmerer, Robin Wall, 152–53

King, Martin Luther, Jr., 198

kingdom of God/heaven, 64, 67, 69, 81–82, 84, 138, 180, 195, 212

Kraybill, Ron, 37

Kreider, Alan, 29, 33

Kreider, Eleanor, 205–6

labeling, 199–100

Law, 124. *See also* Torah

Leatherman, Dan, 145

Lepers (men's group), 74–76

LGBTQ inclusion: congregational and denominational responses vary, 107–8, 121; global church contexts, 186; litmus test for liberal and conservative, 200; parents of gay man speak, 119–20, 127; progressive views on, 145; and same-sex unions, 119–23, 130

listening, 99–100, 103–106, 112

London Mennonite Centre, 103

Lord's Prayer: Amish use, 30–31; daily use, 215; New Jerusalem embodies, 80; pope cites, 176; unity reflected in, 205–6

Luke (Gospel of), 65, 176

Luther, Martin, 181

Lutheran/Mennonite dialogue, 150, 182–83

lynching, 90, 175, 235n13

manifest destiny, 197–98 236n4 (ch. 12)

Mark (Gospel of), 65

March for Life, 19–20

Martyrs Mirror, 182–83

Matthew (disciple), 63–64

Matthew (Gospel of): brood of vipers, 67; conflict instructions, 69, 104–107; make disciples, 180; Sabbath, 123–24; Sermon on the Mount, 30, 65; tax collectors and sinners, 63–64; wise as serpents, 76

Medicine Woman, 156–57

Mennonites: beginnings, 159, 182; diverse, 188–90; World War I aftermath, 184–85

Mennonite Disaster Service, 190–91

Mennonite/Lutheran dialogue, 150, 182–83

Mennonite World Conference, 183–89; controversial issues, 188–89; Shared Convictions of, 185–187

Mesha inscription, 228n2

metanarrative, 196–98, 200

mezuzah, 31–32, 215

Micah (book of), 23, 25, 49–50

Miller, Larry, 183

Millsaps, Cyneatha, 90

Mishnah, 51

missionaries, 127, 140–141

Moore, Osheta, 174–76

moral discernment, 106–7

moral foundations theory, 34–37, 210

Moral Reconation Therapy, 234n4

Moses, 42, 46–49, 158–59

Münster Anabaptists, 181–82

Native American Church, 150

Native peoples, 149, 152, 156, 161. *See also* Indigenous peoples; *and individual people groups*

Neff, Christian, 184–85

Nero (emperor), 78, 143, 201, 232n3 (ch. 7)

Neufeld, Tom Yoder, 190

New Jerusalem, 80–81, 95–96, 212, 229n6 (ch. 4)

news and commentary, 219–20

Nicodemus, 87–89, 230n2

Noko, Ishmael, 182

Northern Ireland, 202–203

nuclear weapons, 94–97, 153, 179

Oklahoma City bombing, 154–55

options for action, 215–17

Orwell, George, 151

Paul (apostle): advocate for Gentiles, 125; angry words, 110, 131–32; appearance, 107; conversion, 232n6; Damascus journey, 127, 139; endangered in

Jerusalem, 142–44; freedom in Christ, 124; persecuted believers, 233n10; Roman citizen, 76–77
parable of wheat and weeds, 84–85
Patrick, Devonte Ray, 165–66
Pax Romana, 58
peace activists, 97–98
Pentecost, 213–14
Peter (apostle), 23, 69, 126, 131–32, 138
Pharisees, 59, 66–67, 89, 126
Philo of Alexandria, 122
Phoebe, 83
Pledge of Allegiance, 77–78, 229n4 (ch. 4)
polygamy, 43
porneia, 232n8
Potawatomi people, 159, 162
Prairie Street Mennonite Church, 165–69
Pray as You Go, 200
Princeton Theological Seminary, 94–95
Prisca (Priscilla) and Aquila, 83
prophecy in church, 108–9
Proverbs (book of), 29

Qumran, 59, 68

racism, 81, 90–91, 93, 109, 151, 165–78
Ray of Hope Foundation, 168
reconciliation, 22, 25, 37, 69–70, 136, 141, 162–63, 182, 200–202, 205, 211, 215
redlining, 172, 178
reparation, 151, 159–62
residential schools, 149–150
resurrection, 64, 110, 136–40, 213
"Return to the Earth" project (burial of Indigenous remains), 159
right remembering, 149–63
Riley, Adrian, 168–70
Rodgers, Ken, 161
Roman Empire, 56–58, 78
Roman-Jewish treaty, 232n3 (ch. 8)
Romans (book of): authorities instituted by God, 76–77; do not pass judgment, 77, 143; exhortation to forbearance, 143; live in harmony, 143, 201; overcome evil with good, 29
Rome as harlot, 78
Rotary Club, 77
Rother, Stanley, 135–36
Rust Belt workers, 92
Ruth (book of), 45–49
Ruth, John L., 234n11
Rwandan massacre, 196–97

Sadducees, 59–60, 64–66, 109

Schloneger, Florence, 159–61
school-to-prison pipeline, 170
2 Corinthians, 111, 177, 200
Septuagint, 232n7
Sermon on the Mount, 30, 82
Shammai (rabbi), 50–52
"Shared Convictions of Global Anabaptists," 186–87
Sharp, Pauline, 160
Shepherd of Hermas, 235n18
Simon the Zealot, 68–69
Skywoman, 152–53
slavery, 60, 79, 151, 173, 198
Solomon (king of Israel), 49
Son of Man, 82, 229n7 (ch. 4), 230n12
spiritual disciplines, 204–205
Stark, Rodney, 235n18
Suetonius, 237n10
sword, Jesus' comments on, 229n8
synagogues, 139–40

Talmud, 50–51, 66
Tanner, Angela, 166–68
Tinker, George, 161
Torah, 41, 47, 51–52, 59, 136, 158
track two diplomacy, 87, 89, 91, 203, 212
tradition (church), 130–31
tribalism, 18–19, 198–99
Trump, Donald, 74, 114
Tz'utujil people, 135–36

United Nations, 179
unity: divine gift, 191; global church, 179–93; Mennonite, 186–87; mission, 207; Paul committed to, 141–44; worship practices for, 205–6

Washita massacre, 155–57
Weaver-Zercher, David, 228n4 (ch. 1)
Wesley, John, 131
whataboutism, 162
White male privilege, 170, 174
White supremacy, 90, 94, 155, 168–69, 174–176
Winthrop, John, 236n3 (ch. 12)
women in church, 82–83, 230n9–10 (ch. 4)
Women's March for Reproductive Rights, 20
World War I, 184
worship practices for unity, 205–206

Yoder, June Alliman, 229n4 (ch. 4)

Zacchaeus, 63–64
Zealots, 60, 68–69

NOTES

INTRODUCTION (pp. 17–26)

1. Suzanne Kapner and Dante Chinni, "Are Your Jeans Red or Blue? Shopping America's Partisan Divide," *Wall Street Journal*, November 19, 2019, https://www.wsj.com/articles/are-your-jeans-red-or-blue-shopping-americas-partisan-divide-11574185777.
2. See, for example, Stephen Hawkins, Daniel Yudkin, Míriam Juan-Torres, and Tim Dixon, *Hidden Tribes: A Study of America's Polarized Landscape* (New York: More in Common, 2018), https://hiddentribes.us/media/qfpekz4g/hidden_tribes_report.pdf.
3. Peter T. Coleman, *The Way Out: How to Overcome Toxic Polarization* (New York: Columbia University Press, 2021), loc. 219 of 6885, Kindle.
4. Thomas R. Yoder Neufeld, *Ephesians*, Believers Church Bible Commentary (Scottdale, PA: Herald Press, 2002), 106–37.
5. For basic conflict transformation practices, see John Paul Lederach, *Reconcile: Conflict Transformation for Ordinary Christians* (Harrisonburg, VA: Herald Press, 2014).

CHAPTER 1 (pp. 27–38)

1. W. Klassen, "Coals of Fire: Sign of Repentance or Revenge?" *New Testament Studies* 9 (1962–63): 337–50.
2. Alan Kreider, *The Patient Ferment of the Early Church: The Improbable Rise of Christianity in the Roman Empire* (Grand Rapids, MI: Baker Academic, 2016).
3. Steven M. Nolt, "Why the Amish Forgave a Killer" (Goshen College Convocation presentation, Goshen, IN, October 1, 2007), https://www.goshen.edu/news/pressarchive/10-02-07-nolt-convo/speech.html.

227

4. How could the Amish be so forgiving toward an outsider and so judgmental toward their own kin who leave the Amish church? Historian David Weaver-Zercher says, "The answer lies in the distinction between forgiveness and pardon. *Forgiveness* refers to a victim's commitment to forgo revenge and replace anger (toward the offender) with love and compassion. *Pardon*, on the other hand, refers to the dismissal of disciplinary consequences." If the killer had not died, the Amish "would have sought to forgive him but nonetheless supported his imprisonment." David Weaver-Zercher, "Amish Grace: How Forgiveness Transcended Tragedy," History News Network, George Washington University, October 2007, https://historynewsnetwork.org/articles/43069.html.

5. James Clear, *Atomic Habits: Tiny Changes, Remarkable Results* (New York: Avery, Penguin Random House, 2018), 16. Clear uses the word *atomic* to mean small, like a single atom.

6. Kreider, *Patient Ferment*, 188.

7. Jonathan Haidt, *The Righteous Mind: Why Good People Are Divided by Politics and Religion* (New York: Vintage Books, Random House, 2012), 65.

CHAPTER 2 *(pp. 39–53)*

1. The earliest known list of our twenty-seven New Testament books appears in the Thirty-Ninth Festal Epistle of Athanasius, bishop of Alexandria, in AD 367. A generation later, ecumenical (global) church councils ratified this list.

2. See, for example, the ninth-century BC Mesha inscription, which tells how King Mesha of Moab slaughtered soldiers and inhabitants of cities conquered in the name of the god Chemesh. William Brown, "Moabite Stone [Mesha Stele]," *World History Encyclopedia*, February 11, 2019, https://www.worldhistory.org/Moabite_Stone_[Mesha_Stele]/.

3. Ancient Israelites technically were *henotheists*, meaning they recognized the existence of multiple gods but worshiped only Yahweh. Bart Ehrman, "Were Ancient Israelites Actually Monotheists?" *Bart Ehrman Blog: The History and Literature of Early Christianity*, January 12, 2021, https://ehrmanblog.org/were-ancient-israelites-actually-monotheists/.

4. Paraphrased by Shoshannah Brombacher, "On One Foot," Chabad, June 20, 2008, https://www.chabad.org/library/article_cdo/aid/689306/jewish/On-One-Foot.htm.

5. Email correspondence with the author, September 4, 2022.

CHAPTER 3 *(pp. 55–71)*

1. Designed by academics associated with the University of California, the study surveyed 8,620 respondents in English and Spanish

in May and June 2022. Grayson Quay, "Poll: Over 50 Percent
of Americans Expect a Civil War 'In the Next Few Years,'"
The Week, July 20, 2022, https://theweek.com/polls/1015291/
poll-over-50-percent-of-americans-expect-a-civil-war-in-the-next-few-years.

2. Josephus, *Jewish War* 5.11.1.

3. The Western Wall is the west side of the massive, raised platform built
by Herod the Great to create a giant courtyard on which the temple and
related buildings stood.

4. Josephus, *Jewish Antiquities* 11.8.3–7.

5. Jews still celebrate this victory every year as the festival of Hanukkah.

6. Seán Freyne, "The Galilean World of Jesus," in *The Early Christian World*,
vol. 1, edited by Philip E. Esler (New York: Routledge, 2000), 113–35.

7. Luke 6:15; Acts 1:13; Matthew 10:4; and Mark 3:18 call this man "the
Cananaean," an Aramaic political term for a Zealot.

8. Jesus surprisingly tells his disciples to take purse, bag, *and sword*. It is
unlikely that Jesus intended the sword to harm people since there is no hint
elsewhere in the Gospels of his endorsing such violence.

CHAPTER 4 *(pp. 73–86)*

1. "About the APS," American Philosophical Society, accessed September 20,
2022, https://www.amphilsoc.org/about.

2. See Caleb Bauer, "Plans Filed for Immigration Detention Center
in Elkhart County," *South Bend (IN) Tribune*, December 5, 2017,
https://www.southbendtribune.com/story/news/local/2017/12/05/
plans-filed-for-immigration-detention-center-in-elkhart-county/45924107/.

3. In Acts 27, Paul is traveling as a prisoner on a Roman commercial vessel,
but he almost certainly was on similar ships during his missionary journeys.

4. A Christian Pledge of Allegiance, in familiar cadences, can serve as an
alternative: "I pledge allegiance to Jesus Christ and to God's kingdom
for which he died, one Spirit-led people the world over, indivisible, with
love and justice for all." June Alliman Yoder and J. Nelson Kraybill,
Voices Together (Harrisonburg, VA: MennoMedia, 2020), 929. Used with
permission.

5. Reformed theologian Karl Barth and Lutheran theologian Hans Asmussen
were authors of the Barmen statement.

6. It is debatable whether Revelation 22:14–15 is rejecting people or practices.
Because of the author's vision of an expansive New Jerusalem, I infer
the latter.

7. The English Standard Version, used here, captures the point I believe the
author of Hebrews is making: Jesus has become the "son of man" under
whose feet Psalm 8 says God "put all things." Some other versions translate
"son of man" (singular in both Psalm 8:4 and Hebrews 2:6) as "human

beings" (plural). For the argument in Hebrews 2:7–9, however, that unhelpfully moves the focus from one person (Jesus) to all of humanity.

8. See Stanley Hauerwas and William H. Willimon, *Resident Aliens: Life in the Christian Colony*, expanded ed. (Nashville: Abingdon Press, 2014).

9. Many interpreters contend that an ancient scribe inserted these words and that Paul did not write them. That is plausible because of the apostle's openness elsewhere to women having public leadership roles.

10. It appears that Paul is speaking here of how men and women function in public worship, since later in the chapter he specifies that his instructions are for "when you come together as a church" (1 Corinthians 11:18).

11. The Greek word here is *synergoi* (literally "workers together"), which the NRSV unhelpfully renders as "servants."

12. See Marlin Jeschke, *Discipling in the Church: Recovering a Ministry of the Gospel* (Scottdale, PA: Herald Press, 1988), 153–62. I question Jeschke's assertion that since Jesus saw the end-times "harvest" as beginning with his ministry, the church must separate wheat and weeds in the present age. Definitive sorting of wheat and weeds happens "when the Son of Man comes in his glory" (see Matthew 25:31–46), leaving unresolved how much sorting the church should attempt now.

CHAPTER 5 *(pp. 87–101)*

1. The high priest Caiaphas, when reminded that the Romans could brutally intervene to stop the Jesus movement, said, "It is better . . . to have one man die for the people than to have the whole nation destroyed" (see John 11:48–50).

2. The Greek text literally says "Are you *the* teacher Israel . . . ?"

3. Cyneatha Millsaps, "Ponder—Why Am I Scared?" *Mennonite Women Voices* (blog), August 12, 2021, https://mennonitewomenusa.org/2021/08/ponder-why-am-i-scared/.

4. Ahmaud Marquez Arbery was shot multiple times and killed on February 23, 2020, in Satilla Shores, Georgia. Three men ultimately were convicted of murder and sentenced to life in prison, two without the possibility of parole.

5. Steven Greenhouse, "Through the Working Class: Five Union Members from across the Rust Belt Reflect on Eroding Faith in the Media," *Columbia Journalism Review*, Winter 2019, https://www.cjr.org/special_report/through-the-working-class.php.

6. Nina J. Easton, *Gang of Five: Leaders at the Center of the Conservative Crusade* (New York: Simon and Schuster, 2020), 155.

7. Quoted in Kermit D. Johnson, *Realism and Hope in a Nuclear Age* (Atlanta: John Knox Press, 1988), 7–8.

8. *Gospel Herald* 76, March 29, 1983, 223.

9. Quoted in Richard K. Taylor, "Of Peace and Policy: A Conversation with a Former Army Chief of Chaplains," *Sojourners*, October 1983, 25–27.

10. Johnson, *Realism and Hope*, 1.

11. Johnson, 2.

12. Valarie Kaur, *See No Stranger: A Memoir and Manifesto of Revolutionary Love* (New York: One World, 2020), 143, 156, 157; quoted in "Holy Listening, Courageous Listening," Center for Action and Contemplation Daily Meditations, July 26, 2022, https://cac.org/daily-meditations/courageous-listening-2022-07-26/.

CHAPTER 6 *(pp. 103–117)*

1. The Greek text of Matthew 18:18 has rare future perfect verbs: "*will have been prohibited* in heaven."

2. Email correspondence with the author, September 5, 2022.

3. William Wright, trans., *Apocryphal Acts of the Apostles*, vol. 2 (1871; repr., Frankfurt: Outlook Verlag, 2022), 117.

4. For a Mennonite adaptation, see "Guidelines for Biblical/Communal Discernment: Commended by the Executive Board for Use in Settings across Mennonite Church USA," Mennonite Church USA, updated June 5, 2015, https://mcusacdc.org/wp-content/uploads/2019/04/MC-USA-Guidelines_for_Biblical_Communal_Discernment.pdf.

5. Victoria G. Curtiss, *Guidelines for Communal Discernment* (Louisville: Presbyterian Peacemaking Program, 2008), 20, https://www.sneucc.org/files/files/documentsnews/discernment-guidelines.pdf.

6. Curtiss, 4.

7. David E. Fitch, *The Church of Us vs. Them: Freedom from a Faith That Feeds on Making Enemies* (Grand Rapids, MI: Brazos, 2019), 1, 11, Kindle.

8. See "Goals of the Colossian Way" at https://colossianforum.org/the-colossian-way-experience/.

9. Quoted in Abigail Ham and Jocelyn Nuñez-Colón, "Partnership with Colossian Forum Paves Way for Campus Conversation about Sexuality," *Chimes*, November 1, 2021, https://calvinchimes.org/2021/11/01/partnership-with-colossian-forum-paves-way-for-campus-conversation-about-sexuality/.

10. Quoted in Corey Nathan and Ronnie Nathan, "Michael Gulker, President of the Colossian Forum, Helps Churches Facilitate Healthier Conversations around Politics," *Talkin' Politics and Religion without Killin' Each Other*, produced by Corey Nathan and Tristan Drew, podcast, 1:14:38, March 3, 2021, https://www.politicsandreligion.us/e/michaelgulker_colossianforum/.

11. "Our Story: Building a House United," Braver Angels, accessed September 20, 2022, https://braverangels.org/our-story/#our-approach.

12. David Blankenhorn, *In Search of Braver Angels: Getting Along Together in Troubled Times* (New York: Braver Angels, 2022), 65.

13. Blankenhorn, 68.

CHAPTER 7 *(pp. 119–133)*

1. Tim Fitzsimons, "40 Percent of LGBTQ Youth 'Seriously Considered' Suicide in Past Year, Survey Finds," NBC News, July 15, 2020, https://www.nbcnews.com/feature/nbc-out/40-percent-lgbtq-youth-seriously-considered-suicide-past-year-survey-n1233832.
2. Names in this story have been changed to protect confidentiality.
3. Emperor Nero, for example, neutered and married a young boy. Suetonius, *Nero 28, Lives of the Caesars.*
4. See William Loader, "Same-Sex Relationships: A First-Century Perspective," *HTS Theological Studies* 70, no. 1 (January 2014), https://hts.org.za/index.php/hts/article/view/2114/4567.
5. For this discussion of Acts 10–15 I am indebted to Luke Timothy Johnson, *Scripture and Discernment: Decision Making in the Church* (Nashville: Abingdon Press, 1996).
6. Paul interprets his conversion in the light of scripture in Acts 26:22–23.
7. The book of Acts quotes scripture from the Septuagint, the Greek translation of the Hebrew Bible. Our English translations of the Old Testament are based directly on the Hebrew Bible. That is why quotes from the Old Testament that appear in our New Testament sometimes do not match Old Testament passages as we find them in our Bibles. Amos 9:11–12 in the Septuagint says, "In that day I will raise up the tabernacle of David that is fallen, and will rebuild the ruins of it, and will set up the parts thereof that have been broken down, and will build it up as in the ancient days: that the remnant of men, and all the Gentiles upon whom my name is called, may earnestly seek, saith the Lord who does all these things."
8. The Greek word here is the broad term *porneia*, which could mean prostitution, unchastity, fornication, or any other kind of sexual immorality.
9. This outline is adapted from my article, "Power and Authority: Helping the Church Face Problems and Adapt to Change," *Conrad Grebel Review* 17, no. 1 (Winter 1999), 17–34.
10. Johnson, *Scripture and Discernment*, 55.

CHAPTER 8 *(pp. 135–147)*

1. See María Ruiz Scaperlanda, *The Shepherd Who Didn't Run*, rev. ed. (Huntington, IN: Our Sunday Visitor, 2019).
2. John Rosengren, "The Good Shepherd," *Notre Dame Magazine,* Summer 2019, https://magazine.nd.edu/stories/the-good-shepherd/.
3. A Roman-Jewish treaty emerged as early as 161 BC (1 Maccabees 8:17–30). But when the Christian offshoot of Judaism expanded and the

movement transcended ethnicity, Rome sometimes viewed the phenomenon as subversive.

4. Josephus, *Jewish War* 5.367.
5. Philo, *Embassy to Gaius* 23 (157).
6. Josephus, *Jewish War* 2.409.
7. Josephus, *Jewish Antiquities* 17.271–87; *Jewish War* 2.56–69.
8. Fourth-century church historian Eusebius tells of Jewish revolts against Rome (AD 115–17) in Cyrene and Egypt. The Roman military killed "many thousands of Jews." *Ecclesiastical History* 4.2.1–5.
9. The Greek word for "nations" here is *ethnoi*, usually translated as "Gentiles" elsewhere in the New Testament.
10. Before joining the Christian movement, Paul himself participated in violence against believers who attended synagogue (Acts 22:19).
11. Josephus, *Jewish Antiquities* 20.51–53.
12. 1 Clement 5:5–7.
13. Tacitus, *Annals* 15.44.
14. Dan Leatherman, letter to the editor, "The Backlash Is Coming," *Anabaptist World*, July 8, 2022, 6.
15. Paul J. Achtemeier, *The Quest for Unity in the New Testament Church* (Philadelphia: Fortress Press, 1987), 2.

CHAPTER 9 (pp. 149–164)

1. Jason Horowitz and Ian Austen, "Pope Apologizes in Canada for Schools That Abused Indigenous Children," *New York Times*, July 25, 2022, https://www.nytimes.com/2022/07/25/world/americas/pope-apology-canada-indigenous.html.
2. Robin Wall Kimmerer, *Braiding Sweetgrass: Indigenous Wisdom, Scientific Knowledge, and the Teachings of Plants* (Minneapolis: Milkweed Editions, 2020), 8.
3. For the story of Betty and Lawrence Hart, and for quotes included here, I am indebted to Raylene Hinz-Penner, *Searching for Sacred Ground: The Journey of Chief Lawrence Hart, Mennonite* (Telford, PA: Cascadia, 2007). Chief Hart died in Oklahoma on March 6, 2022.
4. Hinz-Penner, 115–17.
5. The hymn, with words by Belle Rouse and Frances Goose, appears in *Tsese-Ma'heone-Nemeotȯtse: Cheyenne Spiritual Songs* (Newton, KS: Faith & Life Press, 1982), 152.
6. Rosemary Stephens, "Reflecting Back on Tribal Veteran/Elder Lawrence Hart," *Cheyenne and Arapaho Tribal Tribune* 16, no. 22 (November 15, 2020): 3–5.
7. Hinz-Penner, *Searching for Sacred Ground*, 145.
8. Zoom interview by the author, April 1, 2022.

9. Quoted in Katerina Friesen, ed., *Stories of Repair: A Reparative Justice Resource toward Dismantling the Doctrine of Discovery* (Phoenix: Dismantling the Doctrine of Discovery Coalition, Pacific Southwest Mennonite Conference, 2021), 17.

10. Zoom interview by the author, April 1, 2022.

11. For an example of a descendant of European settlers researching the history of Indigenous people in their home area, see John L. Ruth, *This Very Ground, This Crooked Affair: A Mennonite Homestead on Lenape Land* (Telford, PA: Cascadia, 2021).

12. Terra Brockman, "A Church Returns Land to American Indians," *Christian Century*, March 3, 2020, https://www.christiancentury.org/article/features/church-returns-land-american-indians.

13. To learn more about the historic and present-day Indigenous inhabitants of the place where you live, see a map of Indigenous ancestral territories at Native Land (https://www.native-land.ca).

CHAPTER 10 *(pp. 165–178)*

1. This tragedy happened on December 23, 2013.

2. Joint interview by the author with Angela Tanner and Adrian Riley, March 24, 2022.

3. "Our Vision," Ray of Hope Foundation, November 30, 2021, https://rayhopefoundationmichiana.org.

4. Angela Tanner and Adrian Riley are certified in Moral Reconation Therapy, based on Lawrence Kohlberg's levels of cognitive reasoning. See "MRT—Moral Reconation Therapy," https://www.moral-reconation-therapy.com.

5. See "What Is the School-to-Prison Pipeline?," *Current Events Classroom* (New York: Anti-Defamation League, 2015), https://www.adl.org/sites/default/files/what-is-the-school-to-prison-pipeline.pdf.

6. Not his real name.

7. With his permission, Carter's real name appears here. Carter reviewed this chapter shortly before his unexpected death on October 13, 2022.

8. Many Black Americans have ancestors from West Africa who were enslaved, though a minority of ancestors were indentured servants. A 2014 genetic study found that the average African American genome was almost one-quarter European, and less than 1 percent Native American. Katarzyna Bryc, Eric Y. Durand, J. Michael Macpherson, David Reich, and Joanna L. Mountain, "The Genetic Ancestry of African Americans, Latinos, and European Americans across the United States," *American Journal of Human Genetics* 96 (January 8, 2015): 37–53, https://www.ncbi.nlm.nih.gov/pmc/articles/PMC4289685/. Having European parentage or ancestry did not spare Black people from the devastating effects of slavery and racism.

9. Osheta Moore, *Dear White Peacemakers: Dismantling Racism with Grit and Grace* (Harrisonburg, VA: Herald Press, 2021), 44.

10. Moore, 70.

11. Henry Louis Gates Jr., "The Truth Behind '40 Acres and a Mule,'" *The African Americans: Many Rivers to Cross*, last modified September 18, 2018, https://www.pbs.org/wnet/african-americans-many-rivers-to-cross/history/the-truth-behind-40-acres-and-a-mule/.

12. Robert Fink, "Homestead Act of 1862," *Britannica*, accessed September 20, 2022, https://www.britannica.com/topic/Homestead-Act.

13. NAACP records say there were 4,743 lynchings between 1862 and 1968, though "many historians believe the true number is underreported." Black people were the primary victims, but victims also included immigrants and people who opposed lynching. "History of Lynching in America," NAACP, last modified February 11, 2022, https://naacp.org/find-resources/history-explained/history-lynching-america. The last recorded lynching in the United States occurred in 1981, but families of recent victims and independent researchers assert that lynching continues to this day. DeNeen L. Brown, "'Lynchings in Mississippi Never Stopped,'" *Washington Post*, August 8, 2021, https://www.washingtonpost.com/nation/2021/08/08/modern-day-mississippi-lynchings.

14. Moore, *Dear White Peacemakers*, 138–39.

15. Moore, 175.

16. Raj Chetty, Matthew O. Jackson, Theresa Kuchler, Johannes Stroebel, Nathaniel Hendren, Robert B. Fluegge, Sara Gong et al., "Social Capital II: Determinants of Economic Connectedness," *Nature* 608 (August 1, 2022): 122–24, https://doi.org/10.1038/s41586-022-04997-3.

17. Claire Cain Miller, Josh Katz, Francesca Paris, and Aatish Bhatia, "Vast New Study Shows a Key to Reducing Poverty: More Friendships between Rich and Poor," *New York Times*, August 1, 2022, https://www.nytimes.com/interactive/2022/08/01/upshot/rich-poor-friendships.html.

18. James 2:1–13 discusses issues related to rich and poor worshiping together, and second-century Shepherd of Hermas (*Similitudes* 2.5–7) speaks of reciprocal benefits between rich and poor. See also Rodney Stark, *The Rise of Christianity: A Sociologist Reconsiders History* (New York: HarperCollins, 1997), 29–47.

19. Lawrence Mishel and Jori Kandra, "CEO Pay Has Skyrocketed 1,322% since 1978," Economic Policy Institute, August 10, 2021, https://www.epi.org/publication/ceo-pay-in-2020/.

CHAPTER 11 *(pp. 179–193)*

1. "Pope Francis Affirms Catholic Church's Commitment to the Ecumenical Journey," World Council of Churches News, June 21, 2018, https://www

.oikoumene.org/news/pope-francis-affirms-catholic-churchs-commitment-to-the-ecumenical-journey.

2. Quoted in *Healing Memories: Reconciling in Christ: Report of the Lutheran-Mennonite International Study Commission* (Lutheran World Federation and Mennonite World Conference, 2010), 7, https://www.lutheranworld.org/sites/default/files/OEA-Lutheran-Mennonites-EN-full.pdf.

3. Quoted in *Healing Memories*, 8.

4. See Alfred Neufeld, *Becoming a Global Communion: Theological Developments in Mennonite World Conference from 1925 to 1975* (Asunción: Universidad Evangélica del Paraguay, 2018), 7–34.

5. See John A. Lapp and Ed van Straten, "Mennonite World Conference 1925–2000: From Euro-American Conference to Worldwide Communion," *Mennonite Quarterly Review* 77 (January 2003): 9–14.

6. Neufeld, *Becoming a Global Communion*, 22. The preacher was Jakob Kroeker.

7. Neufeld, 25. The preacher was T. O. Hylkema.

8. Neufeld, 30. The preacher was Pierre Sommer.

9. Zoom conversation with the author, September 2, 2022.

10. Stephen M. R. Covey, *The Speed of Trust: The One Thing That Changes Everything* (New York: Free Press, 2006).

11. Email correspondence with the author, August 31, 2022.

12. Zoom conversation with the author, November 15, 2021.

13. Zoom conversation with the author, November 11, 2021. Harold Friesen has no known relation to Allegra Friesen Epp.

CHAPTER 12 *(pp. 195–208)*

1. Emmanuel M. Katongole with Jonathan Wilson-Hartgrove, *Mirror to the Church: Resurrecting Faith after Genocide in Rwanda* (Grand Rapids, MI: Zondervan, 2009), 34.

2. Katongole, 47.

3. New England preacher John Winthrop in a 1630 sermon used the "city on a hill" metaphor (Matthew 5:14) to describe what he hoped the Massachusetts Bay Colony would become in eyes of the world.

4. "Manifest destiny," an ideology widely purveyed in the United States in the nineteenth century, implied that American people (meaning European immigrants) had special virtues and divine mandate to conquer and rule the North American continent.

5. See Andrew L. Whitehead and Samuel L. Perry, *Taking America Back for God: Christian Nationalism in the United States* (New York: Oxford, 2020).

6. Stephen Hawkins, Daniel Yudkin, Míriam Juan-Torres, and Tim Dixon, *Hidden Tribes: A Study of America's Polarized Landscape* (New York:

More in Common, 2018), https://hiddentribes.us/media/qfpekz4g/hidden_tribes_report.pdf.

7. Katongole, *Mirror to the Church*, 22.

8. Katongole, 18.

9. Interview by the author on April 22, 2022, when Boshart was the faith formation minister for Mennonite Church USA.

10. Suetonius says Claudius "banished from Rome all the Jews, who were continually making disturbances at the instigation of one Chrestus." *Divus Claudius* 25.4. "Chrestus" likely is a reference to Christ. Cassius Dio (60.6.6), on the other hand, says Claudius did not drive Jews out of Rome but forbade them to meet.

11. Quoted in "Ending 30 Years of Mayhem: Lessons from Northern Ireland," *Peacebuilder*, Spring/Summer 2009, https://emu.edu/now/peacebuilder/2009/02/ending-30-years-of-mayhem-lessons-from-northern-ireland/.

12. Email correspondence with the author, June 22, 2022.

13. John L. Bell, "One Is the Body" (Iona: WGRG, Iona Community, 1997, 2002). This and "We Are One in the Spirit" by Peter Scholtes appear in *Voices Together* (Harrisonburg, VA: MennoMedia, 2020), #386 and #387.

14. Interview by the author, July 22, 2022.

CONCLUSION *(pp. 209–214)*

1. Orlando Figes, *The Crimean War: A History* (New York: Metropolitan, 2010), 2.

THE AUTHOR

J. Nelson Kraybill, PhD, was president of Mennonite World Conference (2015–22), president of Anabaptist Mennonite Biblical Seminary in Indiana (1997–2009), and programme director of the London Mennonite Centre in England (1991–96). Author of *Apocalypse and Allegiance: Worship, Politics, and Devotion in the Book of Revelation*, he is an  ordained minister who served churches in England, Vermont, and Indiana. He leads Peace Pilgrim tours to biblical sites in the Holy Land, and currently is teaching and writing in Israel and Palestine (2022-23).